30 DAYS TO UNDERSTANDING OTHER PEOPLE:
A Daily Guide to Improving Relationships

"*30 Days to Understanding Other People* is a great book that gives you incredible insight into why people behave as they do. Beverly is adept at giving practical, daily exercises that help you view other people's 'difficult behavior' in ways that ultimately empower you…thus causing you to respond to common, yet challenging behaviors in much more constructive, fulfilling ways. In this way, it helps you find and exercise your supreme power."

— Cece Suwal & Mark Brener
Co-authors of A Guide to Your Supreme Power,
Co-founders of The One World Initiative

"The critical thing in reading *30 Days To Understanding Other People* by Bev Flaxington is that the information contained within is useful and valuable. This is an easy to read book that's full of content. Getting along with, understanding and cohabitation with others is essential in our personal and professional lives. Each page of this book is packed with gems to guide us along the way to create the best possible relationships and see our part in our endeavors. Highly recommended."

— Debbi Dachinger
Award-winning Syndicated Radio Host, Bestselling Author

"Finding ways to break down the change we want to make is one of Bev Flaxington's specialties. This book offers thoughtful, actionable and easy-to-use ways to learn more about ourselves—and about those around us. Even if you only do a few of the days, it will open your eyes to things you might not have ever thought of before. Do yourself a favor and spend 30 days using this book!"

— Teresa de Grosbois
Bestselling Author and founder of the Evolutionary Business Council

"In our work helping people refer successfully, we know the importance of practicing. In this book, Bev lays out simple ideas in a daily format so that a reader can go along at their own pace, practice with the ideas on a daily basis and start to see change happen in their relationships.

"This book should be by your bedside, on your desk or in your car for constant reference. You CAN influence the change you want to see in your relationships by using these ideas!"

— Tim R. Green
President, Referral Institute of Michigan

30 DAYS TO UNDERSTANDING OTHER PEOPLE:

A Daily Guide to Improving Relationships

Beverly Flaxington

ATA Press

Published by ATA Press
ISBN 978-0-9837620-3-4
Library of Congress Control Number 2012936061
First printing: April, 2012

TABLE OF CONTENTS

This book is dedicated to the three best teachers I've ever had—my children: Samantha, Kiernan and Cynthia.

Thank you for helping me to learn something new every day about myself and about relationships.

INTRODUCTION

Got 30 days to improve your relationships? Sure you do! After all, if you didn't, you probably wouldn't have picked up this book. If I told you I could help you understand other people in 30 days, would you believe me? Well, I can, and if you follow the exercises in this book, you'll learn a lot more about yourself in the process, too.

As a business consultant, hypnotherapist, personal and career coach, author, college professor, corporate trainer, facilitator, behavioral expert, entrepreneur, sales & marketing and business development expert, wife, and mother, I have had an opportunity to interact with people from all walks of life. I find people fascinating and I enjoy learning what others teach me—and then sharing it with people who also want to learn.

Watching people has its benefits. Often, from the outside looking in, we are able to act as sort of armchair quarterbacks and second-guess why a business or personal interaction produces the results it does. The funny thing is that we are rarely able to apply those same principles to our own interactions. Why? I believe that this phenomenon is due to the fact that most of us just don't bother to try to understand why people behave the way they do.

In my first book, *Understanding Other People: The Five Secrets to Human Behavior*, I touched on five of what I believe to be the most important aspects of human behavior. Whether you're in a personal or business situation, people are people, and the fundamentals of why people act as they do don't really change regardless of the arena (of course, business situations might require that we dress our behavior up a bit). Many people have written to ask me, "But how do I understand others more effectively?" My goal with this book is to give anyone who wants it, the insight they need to understand other people, and then allow them to apply this information to their own daily interactions.

Let's face it, some people are just plain hard to understand. I believe that if we can learn ways to understand why people do what they do, we can relax a bit. I find that so many people waste emotional energy because of something someone said or something someone did. One of the nice things about doing the kind of work I do (helping people to understand human behavior) is that I am able to see situations on a daily basis that continually remind me how important it is to help people understand themselves and others.

Understanding other people — truly understanding them in a way that makes us communicate better with them and makes them want to cooperate with us — is very empowering.

The most powerful people are those who understand themselves better than others understand them, and those who understand other people recognize more often why people do things the way they do. This is the type of understanding that allows you to keep calm and cool in your interaction with others, regardless of how difficult or unpleasant that interaction may be.

This book will give you the tools you need to become more powerful by becoming a better communicator, by being able to control your emotions when you communicate with others, and by being in charge of your reactions to others.

Over the next 30 days, your journey will take you through a maze of reasons why so many of our relationships and interactions feel "difficult." We will examine situations where we have the chance to learn about others — and ourselves, too. It's a day-by-day (sometimes hour-by-hour) process that you can start to use today!

A NOTE FROM THE AUTHOR

Most of us know this instinctively that we can't change other people, yet we often can't help but try to change others and fit them into some mold that, we feel, would be "better." The problem with trying to change others is that it can't be done, and so we end up wasting time and energy on a goal that we can never achieve. Being able to let go of the need to change others is so freeing—it frees time and energy for more useful stuff!

While we can't change others, we can certainly change our communication patterns with them. To do that, we need to change our own behavior, or our own reaction to those people.

Saying that we should stop trying to change other people is just like saying "live and let live." What a beautiful idea in theory, but how hard it is for most of us to actually do it! For some reason, humans have this deep need to feel that they are better than others—and what better way to establish that we are "better" than by trying to change or "fix" the other person?

Of course, the result of this need to "fix" someone else leads to many relationship issues and communication problems. Our communication with other people would be much better, and they would appear a lot less "difficult," if we were able to understand a little more about why they do what they do.

So do you want a better relationship? Don't try to change the other person. Instead, accept them and change yourself—not your core values, of course, but the way you communicate with that person. I'll bet you'll find that those "difficult" people would become more accepting of you, and your relationships, both personal and professional, will flourish.

This is what understanding other people is all about.

As you go through the lessons in this book, remember, you have a unique ability to guide your relationships along a course that is smooth and relatively free from conflict. As you read each lesson, apply what you've learned that day (or the next, if you read your lessons in the evening). Practice, practice, practice, and everything will come together by this time next month!

Enjoy!
Beverly Flaxington
Walpole, Massachusetts, February 2012

HOW TO USE THIS BOOK

've arranged a pretty simple setup for you over the next 30 days. Each day, I've included a lesson and an exercise to help you understand others and apply what you've learned to your daily interactions. Whether your focus is on improving work relationships or personal ones, you'll find that by examining these 30 all-too-common experiences, you'll get to know yourself, and others, just a little bit better.

Some of the ways to become better communicators include learning the art of active listening, recognizing and accepting behavioral styles and values that differ from our own, and learning to accept ourselves and others without trying to always be "right" and change others. I've included exercises with each lesson that are designed to highlight what you've learned, and to gently encourage you to look just a little bit differently at the way you communicate.

Lessons
Each day's lesson begins with a brief vignette — an account of something that I have personally experienced and/or witnessed. We learn a lot from what other people go through, and it's often easier to understand something as presented through another person's eyes.

So, to make each lesson easy to understand, I will share a little something with you each day. I'll bet that most of these experiences will strike a chord, because rarely are any one person's experiences so different from those of everyone else. As you read each day's "lesson," I'm sure you'll be able to identify with the subject, since you've probably experienced similar encounters yourself.

Exercises
After you read each lesson, you'll be asked to work on a simple exercise

for the day. These exercises are designed not only to give you insight into how alike we all are, but also to help you understand your role in your relationships with others.

As I mentioned earlier, it's easy to see what others do wrong (or right), but we so often paint ourselves with such a positive brush, we neglect to acknowledge our own shortcomings. Now, there's nothing particularly "wrong" with that. After all, if all we recognized of our own behavior was the bad, we wouldn't be able to live with ourselves. The belief that we're doing the best we can is a self-protective mechanism everyone has that enables them to make it through each day.

But every now and then, each of us takes a step back and says "Wow, maybe I could have done that differently." The exercises you'll encounter over the next 30 days are your opportunity to take that step back and examine your own behavior. The goal is not to make you see that you're a horrible person, but rather that we all make many of the same mistakes, we all have similar reactions in similar situations, and we all have to walk a mile in someone else's shoes, so to speak, in order to understand where they're coming from.

As part of each exercise, you'll be asked to think about a situation that relates to the lesson. Then, and this is very important, you'll be asked to consider what you could do/could have done differently and why that different behavior could potentially change things. Hey, what good is examining behavior if you don't understand the point?

So as you go through each of the exercises, remember, the goal is not to highlight your own bad behavior, but to help you identify with others who may act in a manner that doesn't sit well with you. We've all been there—we've all encountered the "reckless driver" that cuts us off on the highway. But the truth is that most of us have also been that reckless driver—at least in the eyes of other drivers. None of us are immune to bad behavior or poor communication skills.

We're cramming a lot of work into the next 30 days! But by the time you're done, you'll have had at least 30 days of ideas to apply in order to understand other people. You will have in your hands the power to change not only how you interact with others, but possibly how they respond to you, too!

Morning or Evening?

Some of you may prefer reading each day's lesson before you begin your day and applying what you've learned as you go through that day. Others may find it more convenient to read a lesson before bed and apply it to the next day's interactions. Still others may find it best to "backwards apply" the lessons—for instance, you may read a lesson and then think back on your day to examine how the lesson applies to the day you've just finished.

There is no right or wrong way to work through the lessons and activities. Just do what feels right or what makes tackling each lesson most efficient for you. And, as you progress, look for the bonuses for an opportunity to increase your knowledge even more.

Taking a Break

Need to take a break from your lessons? I've numbered the lessons by the day so that you can easily pick up exactly where you left off. So, if something comes up and you can't complete the lessons in the next 30 days, there's nothing wrong with spreading them out a bit.

60-Day Option

For those of you who are real go-getters, I've included a 60-day program option. Extend the program, and what you learn, by applying your newly-formed insight to the next day's interactions. I'll tell you how after each exercise.

Note

I've included a few bonuses at the end of this book. I didn't include them in the first 30 days because they are lessons learned from our furry friends, and although I firmly believe that animals can teach us a lot about each other, I wanted to share these lessons separately for the animal lovers and for those of you who believe in animal intuition.

P.S. If you feel that you'll need more room for recording the day's exercise experiences, pick up a spiral notebook and label each day. Keep this book and your notebook together so that you can refer to each as needed.

week **one**

I **like** **your** **style**

once spent a week in a car with my family. We called it a vacation. We drove many hundreds of miles to see a number of sights. At one point, we had driven for several hours and we were sorely lost in the hill country of Pennsylvania. The kids were starving, the adults were tired, and we decided to stop at a McDonald's for a restroom break and some food. I actually don't usually eat McDonald's food, but my kids like it. Everyone gave me their "order" and then headed off to the restroom.

I approached the counter and was a bit distracted by the sheer number of dining options—Big Mac, or Big Mac meal with what soda, etc.? I walked up to a young lady named Jane and started to place my order. She began to ask me questions—"medium or large", "with or without whipped cream", etc. The kids hadn't given me enough information, so I kept stammering, trying to figure out what to do. In addition, I changed my own mind about whether I should eat there or not, and decided to order something for myself as well.

Throughout the exchange, I remained very respectful of Jane and of how patiently she was waiting for me to respond. At one point I said to her, "Hopefully, I will be your worst customer today and your day will improve from here!" She laughed and said, "You know, usually I would be pretty upset and frustrated that a customer didn't know what they wanted and was holding up the line. But there is something about your style and your approach that I'm not only NOT mad at you, but I am actually enjoying dealing with you!"

I laughed with her and promised to call McDonald's 1-800 number to report what a sweetheart she was (and I did so as soon as I left the location). The exchange with Jane reminded me how much control we have over the many interactions with others we have throughout our day, even though we often forget the power we have to influence other people. I knew I was being annoying, but instead of approaching Jane like she was my servant, I honestly felt respectful toward her and her role. She could feel this from me, and it encouraged her to open up and be more compassionate toward me.

In so many exchanges throughout our day, we are given opportunities to see the humanity in other people. We aren't superior to other people. We aren't better than other people. We are just different. Because our inner experiences often mirror what someone else is dealing with, if I feel frustrated and act out toward you, you will likely become frustrated and respond in kind toward me. But if I truly care about your reaction, and your experience—you might possibly let your guard down and feel more genuine toward me.

This microcosmic experience in a Pennsylvania McDonald's reminded me of how often we want to change another person's behavior in our day-to-day interactions. Instead of expending our energy to change others, what if we changed our own behavior toward someone else? What if we took the reins and decided to be the kinder, gentler person? I'm not advocating that we let someone be abusive—we have to have appropriate boundaries in place, too—but in situations where we might feel someone else was beneath us, what if we acted instead as if they were very important? Seeing the other person as a human being with their own emotional responses can sometimes break down a wall and open up that other person as a real person.

Both Jane and I had an eye-opening experience that day. I don't know if Jane sensed it as I did, but I realized how much power my response had to influence the reaction of another person. If I exerted this power more consciously, I believe I would experience more situations where a person chose a positive response instead of a negative one.

As you work through this week's exercises, be aware of how changing your interactions with other people may involve changing how you conduct yourself. Notice how much more pleasant your day is when you treat others as you would appreciate being treated. Be mindful of how your own behavior affects the way people react to you. Sure, it takes extra time to slow down and act respectfully, but isn't it worth the effort?

day | one | me | first | !

"In the end, the only thing that matters to you, is you and the only thing that matters to me, is me."

— Andrew Ryan, *Bioshock*

once attended a concert with my youngest daughter and my nieces. While we were waiting in line (a long, long line at that…), a man and his young son pushed their way through the crowd to get in front of everyone. One of the other dads in line said quite loudly, "Me first, huh? What makes you so special?"

Later that week, as I was sitting in traffic at a construction area waiting to get to my exit, a car drove along the breakdown lane, blocking all of us trying to exit. A man yelled out of his window, "Hey, jerk—get out of the way; what makes you think you are the only one that matters here?"

The next week, at an amusement park, my husband and I were standing in line with our children when a big boy came from behind and pushed all of the other kids out of the way to get to the ride. My son turned to me and said, "How come he can't wait like everyone else, Mom?"

ME first!! Why is it that some people feel entitled to cut a line, drive around traffic, or push their way to the front as if the rest us simply don't matter? What is inside of these folks that makes their inner voices say, "I shouldn't have to be like everyone else and wait!"

Let's be honest; deep down we all feel like we should get to the front of the line faster than anyone else. We all have our reasons—a sick child at home, a long day, a depressed state of mind, a martyr attitude that has worn me out. How many times has the prospect of a long wait tempted you to push your way to the front of the line? The problem is that if we all have this attitude, who is going to be left to actually wait in line?

In our culture, it is very true that the squeaky wheel gets the oil. Very often, the person who sits and waits patiently is overlooked while someone who raises a fuss gets immediate attention. Many people are taught that it's better to speak up, to be a bit pushy and to let our needs be known. But in many cases, we take our own assertiveness too far. We ignore the fact that other people matter too, and we really aren't any more deserving or important than they are.

What can we do differently to help us understand that maybe we shouldn't always get to the front of the line first? We have to begin by having compassion for other people. We tend to view the people waiting patiently as having little humanity. They are just someone in our way, not a living, breathing, feeling person. And yet, if that person turned out to be a friend or relative or neighbor, wouldn't we be a bit embarrassed that we pushed by them to get in front? Of course we would! We wouldn't want to be seen as a pushy, aggressive, nasty person. Then why is that okay when we are dealing with strangers?

What if we didn't treat others as if they were strangers? What if we treated everyone with kindness and interest in their well-being—as if they were someone we cared about... someone we knew? Instead of seeing the person in the car in front of me as a non-person, I could actually pretend it was someone I cared about. If I did, I might not be so quick to push my way ahead of them.

* EXERCISES *

Today, when you find yourself in a situation where your inner voice cries "ME first!" try to personalize the crowd. Pretend the people around you are people you know and people you care about. See if it changes your approach.

Chances are that today you will experience at least one "ME first!" moment. Whether it's the urge to push your way to the front of the line or the desire to take 15 items into the "10 items only" line, catch yourself about to do it and decide to stop! You don't have to have actually acted on your "ME first!" urge, you just have to acknowledge it.

Record today's "ME first!" moment. Don't think you had one today? Think again. Really look at what you did and felt today. Did you see someone rushing for the sandwich cart and rush to get there first so that they didn't snag the last turkey sandwich? Did you spy some guy heading for the closest seat on the train and walk a little faster so you could get there first?

After you record your "ME first!" moment, write a few sentences about what you could have done differently to change your behavior.

* 60-DAY OPTION *

Tomorrow, apply what you can do differently to a "ME first!" moment.

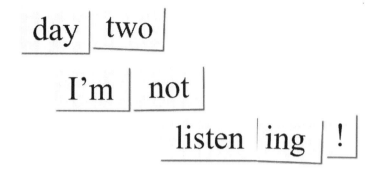

day | two

I'm | not

listen | ing | !

"I know that you believe you
understand what you think I said,
but I'm not sure you realize that
what you heard is not what I meant."

– Robert McCloskey

One of my favorite songs is "I Can't Hear You No More," by Helen Reddy. Grammatically incorrect title aside, this song is a great summary of what often happens between two people who are trying to communicate. In the song, Helen sings to someone over and over again that she can't hear him "no more." It's clear that she's either frustrated by what he's saying, or he's been saying the same thing for so long it's now falling on deaf ears.

Many times, differences in behavioral styles contribute to this problem. If I am a fast-paced, fast-moving, and fast-thinking person, someone who is slower, more methodical, and more thoughtful is going to annoy me. Rather than tell them of my annoyance, I will likely just stop listening; I may put my attention on something else, or I may just tune them out. Conversely, if I am someone who needs time to think and process, and I am interacting with someone who is pushing ideas at me quickly and furiously, I will need to mentally step back so that I can stop the seeming onslaught of words coming at me.

We aren't always conscious that we are doing this—it's our reaction to someone who is very different from us. When behavioral styles don't match, instead of using the energy to figure out how to match ourselves, we will just resist the other person.

Another reason we may not be able hear others is that, in many cases, we are simply on overload: I am multi-tasking and paying little attention to what you might be saying. At any given moment, most of us have information coming at us from email or voice mail, and over the computer or television. We are IM'ing and texting and generally expected to respond in a fairly immediate fashion. I was in someone's office the other day and they were on a conference call, reading emails, preparing a paper they needed to present, AND talking to me. But were they really talking to me? How could that person possibly be focused on what I was saying? Because I knew the person well we were able to joke about it, but it was a great caricature of how many of us operate these days. Slowing down and taking time to listen and focus on another person seems like a lost art.

The problem with this inability to hear one another is that we aren't connecting. We aren't given a chance to have a real understanding of the person who is underneath what's being said. If we rush through our conversations, and we don't pay attention to the emotional side of what's being said, we really don't give ourselves a chance to learn about that person. I read an article about a young person who recently attempted suicide and they said, "It just didn't seem like anyone was listening to me." This is an extreme case, but many of us feel like we interact daily but we don't really connect.

Talking and connecting are two very different experiences.

On a recent trip back home from Houston, TX, I sat next to a lovely woman who was traveling back home to sell her house in Boston. She was talking to me about some of the trials and tribulations she had experienced. It occurred to me, as I listened to her, how tired I was feeling, and how much energy it took for me to stay focused on what she was saying. Her personal pain was clear and I felt it was important for her to seek connection, but it did require me to give from my own emotional reservoir.

I think this is what happens to us sometimes. To truly connect, to really listen, requires tremendous energy; we have to focus. We have to assimilate and engage in active and reflective listening. Sometimes we just don't want to be bothered.

---

* EXERCISES *

Today, pick an interaction or two where you really want to invest your time and attention. See whether the richness of your connection and the feeling you get from true understanding form enough of a payoff that the next time you may be more likely to give more of yourself.

We all do it. We're so busy multitasking that we don't really devote our full attention to anything or anyone. Think you're not guilty? How many times did you check your phone for messages while your spouse was telling you about his/her day? Were you thinking about a response while you were having a disagreement, instead of listening to what the other person had to say? Did you wonder what the time was when your child was regaling you with a tale about his/her day?

* 60-DAY OPTION *

Tomorrow, apply what you can do differently to give your full attention to someone else.

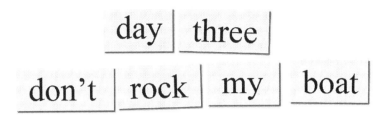

day | three

don't | rock | my | boat

"Son, if there's one thing this life has taught me, it's to avoid trouble and just say nothing. Don't rock the boat. Don't even get in the boat! Just buy some ice cream and walk around the pier."

– Homer Simpson

It's a reality for most of us that we desire harmonious relationships, but we don't always have them. Why is this? Well, it's because the people around us just refuse to behave in the manner we think they should behave. In fact, if all of the people around us would just be like us, do what we want them to do, and act in ways that allow us to stay within our comfort zone — all would be well! Why don't people understand they need to accommodate our desires and make life easier for everyone?

Well, you know the answer — if I want you to be like me, but you want me to be like you…whose idea of harmony should we settle into? Think of the amount of money spent on career counselors, marriage counselors, business coaches, and "renew-our-relationship" workshops. We're all in search of the secret to getting the other person in our life — be it a romantic relationship or a business one — to just behave. We hope and wait for the other person to have their transformation and start doing what we need and want them to do!

But if everyone is trying to keep their own boat stable, and they don't want someone else coming along and making waves, how are we all going to fit in the ocean? The fact is that there are a whole lot of boats in the ocean, and we all have to navigate the waters as peacefully as possible. The uncomfortable feelings that are created when we are in a relationship with someone else are actually there to teach us. The waves can be an indicator of how sturdy our boat really is—how well it can withstand an impending storm and how seaworthy it is. Never rocking the boat lulls one into a false sense of "all is well."

Relationships that are harmonious are wonderful. My closest friend from childhood, Carole Ann, and I have that—we haven't had one fight in all of our decades as friends. It's a great feeling to know someone and know that they really know you too! These relationships don't come along often, and it's important to celebrate and cherish them.

But in many cases, a difficult relationship can teach us something. When we react with difficulty to another person, instead of thinking "How can I fix them?" we might want to ask "What is this person teaching me about me?"

Did you ever stop and think why the loud and obnoxious person in the movie theater or restaurant upsets you? Why the person who cuts you off in traffic is a "jerk"? Why the person who won't return your phone calls frustrates you? Do people engage in behavior that is difficult and bothersome—of course they do! But because we can't stop these individuals from rocking our boats, what we need to do is reflect on our own reactions and wonder what their behavior triggers within us.

Learning about, and learning how to manage, our triggers gives us more personal power. If I don't recognize that your "bad" behavior pushes some sort of button within me, and I just react to it and ruminate on it, I'm wasting my own valuable time and emotional energy. Think about it; is someone else's poor behavior something on which you want to waste your time?

I know I've wasted countless hours over the years, before I understood these concepts, fuming over what someone did, or didn't do, and thinking about how I would react and respond to them the next time I saw them. But the trick isn't to avoid addressing the things that bother us, it's that we need to find respectful and productive ways to bring up things that matter and might enhance our relationships—when we can, and when the other person makes room for us to do so.

Reacting gives us a clue that there is something in us that the other person sets off. What is it and why is it there? Can we learn anything from it that might allow us to grow and develop for the better?

The people who stay in their boat in the safe harbor never get the exhilaration of the open seas. They don't explore, they don't learn new navigation, and they don't become expert at managing their craft. When you will allow your boat to be rocked, and not force the rocking to stop but rather explore what the rocking is about—you can't help but learn something about yourself.

* EXERCISES *

Today, let go of your resistance to others' style and instead use your energy to explore you. What are your triggers? Use your new awareness to take stock of where you are, and decide whether you want to stay there, or go someplace else.

Think you're calm Carl or steady Suzy? Chances are you've got triggers just like the rest of us, whether it's the way your husband chews his mashed potatoes, your daughter's habit of leaving the shower curtain open, or the nasty habit your coworker has of constant pen clicking.

Write about a situation during which one of your triggers caused you to react. What could you have done differently? Why?

* 60-DAY OPTION *

Tomorrow, apply what you can do differently to avoid letting your triggers set you off.

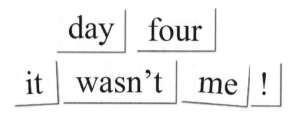

day | four
it | wasn't | me | !

"I didn't do it, nobody saw me do it,
there's no way you can prove anything!"

– Nancy Cartwright

As a mother of three kids, I hear "It wasn't me!" whenever something in the house goes wrong. One of the residents of my house is a mysterious ghost who leaves towels on the floor and food on the counter for the dogs to get, and forgets to feed the cats. We adults laugh at the stories we share about how kids deny responsibility for things they obviously do, but how funny is it when we do this as adults?

Once, overtired and on my way to my daughter's all-day dance recital, I almost ran into another car leaving a parking lot. The other driver luckily swerved to avoid hitting me — but then he turned his car around and chased me, gunning his engine and driving close to my bumper. I was scared, to say the least, but most importantly, I found myself thinking "It wasn't ME that did that...."

The reality? Of course it was me. It was a moment of distraction that thankfully ended well and without injury (except to my nerves and to my pride). The experience also served as a reminder of how easy it is to point the finger at someone else and judge them, not realizing that, in many situations, we are the culprit and the problem.

Most of us like to think we are above reproach. We believe that we make the right decisions, behave in the right ways, and do right by others. If asked, few people would willingly admit they ever drive distracted or put themselves, and others, in jeopardy.

But the truth is that we all make mistakes. We make small mistakes, and sometimes we make really, really big mistakes. Given that most of us can admit, no matter how perfect we believe we are, that we make mistakes, why is it so hard for us to allow someone else to make them? We might absolve ourselves by offering an excuse—in the above example, my daughters were in the car with me; one was yelling at me, and the other one was complaining that her bagel we'd just bought wasn't toasted right, so I admit I was a bit distracted—but, ultimately, who was the one who committed the infraction? Me. It didn't really matter about the why or the how; what mattered was that it happened, and it humbled me for the next time I get ready to throw a mental dagger at another driver who isn't paying attention.

Should we all do a better job of being more attentive when we drive? Sure. Did I learn a valuable lesson about being more careful—especially when I have precious cargo? Sure. But did it also remind me that I do dumb things and need to be more mindful of a judgment I might throw at someone else doing something equally dumb? Absolutely! It's so easy to see clearly when it is the other person's problem, and yet, when we make mistakes, we excuse them away.

Now, I haven't met many people who like to do dumb things and who fare well when severely criticized. Perhaps it is a filter we carry from childhood, but most of us like to do things "right" and avoid getting into trouble. When the car I almost hit began tailing me, it was hard because I knew I had done something wrong and was "guilty." Instead of being angry and indignant, I was actually chagrined because of my behavior.

* EXERCISES *

Today, as you go through your day, remember two important lessons; one is that there is nothing more powerful you can give to others throughout your day than your attention. Release yourself from distractions wherever you can, so you can concentrate on what's important—the task at hand. The other is to remember that you are human, and so is everyone else around you. Find a way to sympathize with someone today over their own bad behavior, and admit a bad behavior you may have engaged in to someone else. The humbling experience can be a healthy one!

Think you're exempt from "It wasn't me!" syndrome? Wrong! Next time you roll through a stop sign because you're distracted while someone else waits patiently, remember, you're "that" guy/gal!

Write about a situation during which you intentionally or unintentionally acted like "that" person, but automatically blamed it on someone else. What could you have done differently? Why?

* 60-DAY OPTION *

Tomorrow, apply what you can do differently to either avoid acting like "that" person or to understand how someone else might do something really stupid but not do so intentionally.

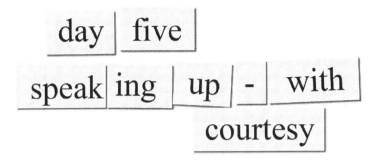

day | five
speak|ing | up | - | with
courtesy

"He who does not have the courage to speak up
for his rights cannot earn the respect of others."

– Rene G. Torres

My son came home from the first day of sixth grade and the first words out of his mouth were, "I HATE art, Mom! It's the worst class ever." I was so shocked to hear this, because he has always been a very good artist and has had his work displayed in the Town Hall and at various art functions around town. I tried to get him to explain why the sudden dislike for the subject, but he wouldn't open up more than this.

Fast-forward to Parent-Teacher Night: I knew I would have the opportunity to talk with a variety of teachers, and I asked my son who I should see. "Just don't go see Mrs. M., my art teacher," he said to me. "I HATE her, she is awful." Of course, I made the decision right then to seek out Mrs. M. that evening so I could take stock of her for myself. I had already made up my mind that I would meet this negative person who wasn't very nice. I waited outside her room and heard her talking with other parents. Instead of what I expected, she was an engaging, upbeat, enthusiastic woman. When it was my turn to talk to her, I introduced myself and laid my cards on the table: "My son, who has always loved art, absolutely hates this class, and I would like to understand why." Mrs. M. was completely taken aback, and we talked in detail about the class, about my son, and about the content of the course.

Come to find out, Mrs. M. is deaf in one ear and the class has over 30 children. When the noise level gets too high, she can't hear anything, has headaches, and generally finds it difficult to function. When the students won't keep the noise to a dull roar, she tells them "NO TALKING!" at all. Now, my son is a social bug and loves to interact with anyone who offers a listening ear. Of course he hates this class—he can't talk.

When I spoke with my son and explained Mrs. M.'s condition, he felt badly. "Why didn't she just tell us?" he replied. My thought was that he made sense; if she did explain it to the class, they might be a bit more sympathetic and responsive. In any event, after I spoke with her, she started treating this class very differently. Now my son enjoys art again and likes the class very much.

What's happening here? It's a common occurrence, in my experience, to assume something about someone else. We don't speak to them, in a courteous manner, to get to the bottom of what's going on. Instead, we stew, we get angry, and we end up disliking being around that person altogether. And yet sometimes, if we would just take the time to talk to the person and explain what we need, the other person will respond.

Why is it so hard for so many people to just speak up? I think it's because most of us don't ever really learn how to communicate a negative experience. My son was mortified to find out I had talked to the teacher: "Mom! What if she talks to me about this? Everyone will know you said something!!" As a sixth grader, he doesn't want to look like he is letting his mom step in to talk to a teacher—that's not cool! But he liked the outcome. He likes the fact that Mrs. M. is now much more agreeable and pleasant in class.

Maybe we avoid bringing up negative issues simply because we don't want to be identified as a trouble-maker. Maybe we haven't learned to be in touch with what is really bothering us, so we just decide we "hate" the person we can't communicate with. Maybe we haven't learned how to deliver negative news and we were told, "If you can't say something nice, don't say anything at all." Whatever the reason, the key to being heard is to learn new behavior.

* EXERCISES *

Today, practice being in touch with what triggers your negative reactions. Consider what's happening and whether there is an opportunity to courteously explain your position to the person or people who bother you. Can you address something and change an outcome in a kind and relational way? Try it—you might be able to effect more change than you think possible!

Think you never act according to how you feel you're being treated? Think again! Did you ever find yourself thinking that sourpuss bank teller wasn't showing us her worst side, but was rather in a lot of pain after spraining an ankle? Or maybe your friend who didn't bother saying goodbye after a minor spat was just distracted, not rude?

Write about a situation during which you encountered someone who seemed determined to ruin your day. How did you react? What could you have done differently? Why?

* 60-DAY OPTION *

Tomorrow, apply what you can do differently to an encounter with someone who seems to be out to get you. Does your newfound insight change the way you react?

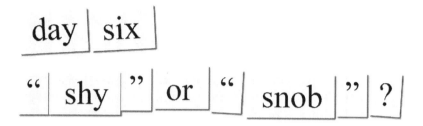

day | six

" | shy | " | or | " | snob | " | ?

> "No one would talk much in society, if he knew how often he misunderstands others."
>
> – Johann Wolfgang von Goethe

I am very fortunate to live near where I grew up, so I am able to periodically see friends from my school days. Some of us get together from time to time and we have been very supportive of one another — especially when we lost one of our group to a sudden heart attack a couple of years ago.

One evening when we were having drinks, one of the women said to me, "Why were you such a snob when we were in school? You would never talk to anyone, you were so stuck-up!" I was stunned by her comment! It actually took me a while to reconcile what she had said with my actual experience in school. When I was in school, particularly in high school, I was terribly shy. I was so shy that I would actually hide in the stairwells when I saw certain people coming down the hall. I had a core group of friends that I could be myself with, but for the most part, I kept to myself. This is hard for people who know me now to believe — as now I am a person who enjoys speaking in front of hundreds, if not thousands, of people. But in those days, I was quiet, timid, and afraid to speak.

This woman's perception of me made me think again about how we view the behavior of others. She saw me as making a choice not to interact with her. She viewed me as rude, or snobby, or stuck-up—like I thought I was better than her and that she was not worth my time. The opposite was really the truth: I was afraid to speak to her—and to most people. I dreaded going into new classes or to lunch if I didn't have someone there whom I knew for support. My entire high school experience was one of trying to hide!

We go through our days so unaware of the labels we apply to other people's behavior and the filters through which we view what others do. When someone you know walks by you and doesn't speak, do you ever find yourself thinking, "What's with her—why isn't she talking to me?" or do you think, "She must not have seen me. She must be so involved in her thoughts." When someone cuts you off in traffic do you think, "What a rude and insensitive jerk!" or do you think, "That person must be trying to get somewhere fast!" We see a certain behavior and instead of assuming the best, or just seeing it as data, we use our imagination to create a negative idea about that person or that event.

Does this mean that there are no rude people? That the person who cut you off wasn't a "rude jerk"? Not necessarily. It just means that we simply don't know what's going on with another person, but we don't give them the benefit of the doubt. I often wonder, if we were to assume the positive, would it actually change our experience? I think it would—we would have different expectations, different understandings, and therefore different experiences.

* EXERCISES *

Today, try to catch yourself when you label someone else's behavior. Be objective about the label you apply. Is there another way to understand what that person is doing and why? Change your filter, change your experience, and see if it changes what you think about another person.

We all need to walk a while in someone else's shoes every now and again; not a mile necessarily, but a good distance. There isn't one of us who hasn't been guilty of snapping at someone because we're having a bad day, ignoring someone because we're distracted, or barreling over someone emotionally because our own emotions are in an uproar. Many times, we do this without even realizing what we've done—only to think we behaved pretty badly.

Write about a situation during which you encountered someone who was just plain rude! How did you react? Even better, write about a situation today where YOU were the rude one. Why did you act that way? What could you have done differently? Why?

* 60-DAY OPTION *

Tomorrow, apply what you can do differently to the next rude person you meet, or to avoid being rude to someone else.

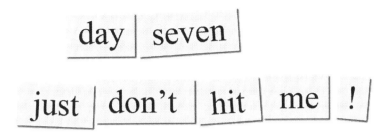

day | seven

just | don't | hit | me | !

"If you approach something differently, you
always have to expect a headwind."

– Jürgen Klinsmann

M y son had to read a book called *The Revealers* for summer reading. He and I took turns; he read a couple of chapters to me,
then I read one to him. It made the story come alive and gave us
something to do together. This book intrigued me because it was about
Russell, a boy who is bullied. Russell seeks out other bullied kids to try
to figure out how to push back on the bullies. At one point, Russell asked
a bully, "Why me?" Russell wanted to know why the bully targeted him
specifically. The bully's reaction? He punched Russell so hard that he fell
to the ground and couldn't see straight.

I thought this scenario was a great way to teach others how to deal
with difficult people. While we may say we are trying to learn different
ways to approach others, to be more attentive and compassionate and less
emotional, sometimes inside we are saying, "I hope my actions make that
other difficult person change!" What we really want is for the other person
to just be different. Russell learned that, by taking a different approach,
he paid a price.

Given that this was a sixth-grade reading assignment, I'm sure that you can guess that Russell figured out how to deal with the bullies and the reader learned some important lessons by the end of the book. But Russell really was experiencing one of the realities of life: We may change. We may approach others differently. But there's no guarantee that the other person will change; sometimes the reaction we expect is not the one we get.

When we seek to deal with difficult people and improve our relationships, we have to give up our desire to change them. We need to consider that it's our energy and our emotions and our focus that become negative in dealing with others who upset us. If we examine our own intentions at times, we're not setting out to change the other person and find the key to unlock their reactions to us; we're setting out to find new ways to give ourselves freedom from the negative reaction.

In other words, it's a bit of self-interest that can sometimes translate into compassion. Refusing to react in the same old ways is more about conserving energy for the positive things we want to accomplish or pay attention to in our lives than it is about a quest to change others.

Be honest with yourself, if you choose to approach someone differently, about why you are doing it. Place your focus on learning, not on trying to gain an advantage. And remember Russell: He genuinely just wanted to understand why he was being bullied, and he got a fist in the nose as a result. While hopefully this won't happen to many of us, we may get emotionally punched out during the process.

If we want to learn from this work, we have to be prepared for anything and give up our expectations that we'll "fix" anyone. We can deal with trying to change ourselves and our reactions. That, alone, takes a tremendous amount of focus and commitment.

* EXERCISES *

Today, to quote Mahatma Gandhi, see if you can "be the change you want to see in the world" and leave the other person's reactions and approaches up to them.

Have you ever noticed how a simple disagreement can explode into something catastrophic? By the time you realize what's going on, your teenage daughter won't talk to you, your coworkers think you're a prima donna, or your spouse sleeps on the couch. Before a disagreement gets out of hand, think about what you can do to keep things from escalating. The reality is that your behavior has a lot to do with how other people behave. Your mother was right when she said "it takes two to tango."

Write about a situation that produced the same old results. What was your role? What could you have done differently? Why?

* 60-DAY OPTION *

Tomorrow, apply what you can do differently to the next situation you encounter that you anticipate will end the same way it always does. Try to change the outcome by changing the way you respond.

week two

the difficult ones

'm often called upon to do a little extra coaching during the holiday months. The most common request I get is to help people deal with difficult relatives or difficult co-workers. The holiday table may be set, but many people don't want to sit at it with their relatives. The holiday work party may be in a fancy location, but some folks don't want to attend and deal with co-workers they don't enjoy being around.

Do difficult people actually become more difficult during the holidays, or are we generally just more stressed and less tolerant of others?

First, let's define "difficult." One radio personality said to me, "What about those loud and boisterous co-workers that you just wish would shut up?!" Let's examine this a bit—should we assume that "loud and boisterous" is negative to everyone? For some people, "loud and boisterous" translates as "outgoing, upbeat, and enthusiastic." Remember, our own behavioral styles determine how we interpret the actions of others; we view others through our own lens. If you aren't like me, I don't particularly like you. I think you should change your behavior—to the way I like to do things!

At one time in my corporate career, I attended many a holiday party where a certain senior executive always acted inappropriately toward the women in the firm. We knew it was going to happen, so no one was surprised when this guy lived up to his reputation. This type of scenario is exactly why we all need to prepare in advance to deal with people we find to be difficult. You know what someone is likely to do that upsets you, so have a plan before you ever walk through the door. My female colleagues and I developed a signal for each other when we needed to be saved from the philandering senior exec. It actually became kind of fun, like a game—so even when he did his thing, instead of getting upset, we put our plan into play!

The truth is, any one of us has the right to have a different response to people who annoy us. We can choose to let such people trigger a bad reaction, or we can decide "Not this time!" I like to mentally imagine myself as a duck when I am dealing with someone who is particularly unpleasant. As the person is talking, I imagine their words rolling down my body as water does off the duck's back. The words fall to the floor, where I can mentally stomp on them while the person keeps talking. I know I might not be able to change that person, but I can choose not to let what he/she is saying soak in and ruin my day.

Prepare for those times you know you will be tested. Know that, at certain times, your defenses may be down to start with, and you may not be able to think on the fly and react quickly. Because of this—prepare. Put on your duck clothes before you walk into a party, meeting, or other situation where you anticipate dealing with someone you find difficult.

As you go through the exercises this week, remember, don't let the difficult people ruin your day—you can find joy in spite of them; all you have to do is look for it!

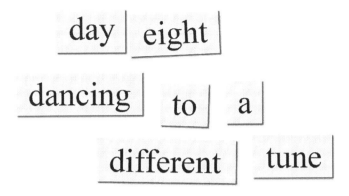

day | eight

dancing | to | a | different | tune

"Insanity is repeating the same mistakes and expecting different results."

– Rita Mae Brown

There is a strong interest, for most people in personal and business situations, in learning how to deal with difficult people. Since teaching others how to deal with difficult people is part of my job, I often find myself talking about the "dance" we get into with others.

The dance goes like this: My sister says something she always says that irritates me, I respond the way I always do that irritates her, she responds the same way again, and so on. We dance the same steps to the same tune over and over again.

Did you ever stop and wonder why we do this? After all, if you know that someone or something irks you, why do you continue to respond in the same way? If you both continue the same dance, do you honestly believe the moves are going to change—will the response from the other person be different? It's silly, isn't it—we know nothing will change, but we stick with what we know.

What happens when you decide to change one step in the dance? I will never forget a time in my marriage where my husband and I had an issue that came up time and time again. We would always respond to each other the same way and, predictably, the issue was never resolved. One day, instead of responding in frustration as he always did, my husband responded with compassion: "I know this is a tough discussion for you. What can we do differently this time so we don't get stuck?"

Huh?! His response knocked me right off my feet. I couldn't even answer him at first, and when I did, it was in a much more thoughtful and caring manner.

When my husband responded differently—treated me, and the situation, differently, and changed the dynamic—he altered my way of dealing with the matter too. I always tell people that we can't change others... much to our chagrin. But the truth is that when WE change, others often change in response.

If we take a different step on the dance floor, the other person is forced to take a different step, too. They may not step where we want them to, but we can be assured it won't be the same steps they've always taken.

It's always a good idea to practice dancing to a different tune. We know what issues bug us. We have to learn to identify the dances we are likely to waltz into as we go about our lives, and make a conscious decision to dance to a different drummer!

* EXERCISES *

Today, take a few minutes to identify those relationships that challenge you or cause you some sort of difficulty. Can you close your eyes and replay a past discussion where someone said something, you responded, and then the dance began? Remember how it went? Be prepared by knowing, so that when you greet that person again, and she or he says or does the thing that always sets you off, you will be prepared. Prepare your game plan in advance so instead of being robotic and reactive (as we often are in relationships), you can be proactive and ready to respond in an entirely new fashion.

None of us are exempt from engaging in the same old song and dance. We have the same old arguments with family members, take the same old position during a disagreement, and react in the same old way when our kids challenge us. And we do this knowing that we'll end up in the same place we always end up.

The insane thing about this is that most of us realize that just one little variation in the dance will produce different results. We tend to instinctively know that if we refuse to engage, the results will be different, but we still follow that path right down the road to frustration.

Bonus: It can be fun to think about the situations where you'll use your newfound dancing shoes. When you imagine each situation that involves the same old dance, imagine what you can do or say to change the steps.

Write about a situation that would normally call for the same old dance. What could you have done differently? Why?

* 60-DAY OPTION *

Tomorrow, apply what you can do differently and focus on dancing a different dance.

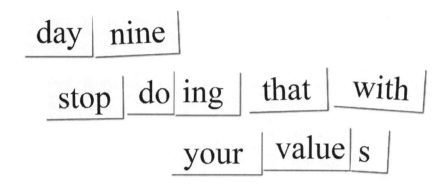

day | nine

stop | do | ing | that | with | your | value | s

"What we have here is a failure to communicate."

– Paul Newman, *Cool Hand Luke*

I have a client that recently acquired another company. My client and the new company are trying to integrate practices, ideas, and ways to work together by bringing two separate units together into one. As I work with the management of this newly combined company, I am reminded of how critical knowing another person's values and trying to refrain from making a "values" judgment really is.

In this case, the leaders of the existing firm are very smart people who love to learn, love to think and investigate, and enjoy new information. The problem is, when it comes time to make decisions, the intellectual exercise of learning and thinking gets in the way.

My client believes that all company decisions should have a mostly positive impact on the employees of the newly combined firm. No one should lose a job, even though there is a great deal of redundancy all over the new organization.

So, in my consultant role I am left with a quandary. I want to make decisions and help move things along—and the employees seem to want this, too. But management wants to be more thoughtful and consider many options before they act. I'm trying to find ways to organize the firm effectively, but I have to do it with two people in many roles so as to avoid leaving anyone out in the cold!

I applaud the values the managers hold and believe in them too, but I find myself getting into trouble every time I want to make a decision. One leader calls me "pushy" in my approach.

So I am reminded of the importance of values—while almost everyone I work with values what I value, there are also times when I find myself in new territory with several leaders who don't hold my number-one value at all.

These types of situations force me to reconsider how I make a suggestion, what steps I take, and how fast I take them. I realize that the ultimate goal is to give this company what they need, and what will work for them—not for me. I must keep stepping back and questioning what I am doing, asking myself "Who needs this—me or them?" If I catch myself pushing my own values, I have to regroup and re-examine what I am proposing, to make sure it fits the value framework I am working within at the moment.

Situations like this are very helpful because they force me to practice many of the techniques I espouse. In this case, I am finding myself in an "Interested Observer" mode trying to see how what I say is received—and when it isn't received, trying to find another way to be helpful.

Be watchful of values disconnects. When someone accuses you of something, or doesn't seem to understand what you are saying or doing, it's oftentimes because you are acting from values that matter to you—and they may be different values from the person observing you and your decisions. Values run very deep—we can't change them, but we can be aware of them. In all communication with others, awareness alone is a gift we can give.

* EXERCISES *

Today, as you go through your day, observe how your values affect the way you interact with others. Examine a few situations and determine if your values, or the other person's values, led the interaction. How respectful are you of other people's values? Do you force your values into a situation, or do you allow each interaction to be guided by the appropriate values—whether those values are yours, another person's, an organization's, etc.?

It's completely human to allow your own perceptions of the world to take over when interacting with others. After all, it's what we have experienced that colors the way we look at things, and therefore, the way we act. But if everyone approached every interaction with nothing in mind but their own desires, perceptions, and morals, then we would all be in a heap of trouble! Take a moment to think about how you can change your interactions by respecting the values of others.

Write about a situation during which you let your values lead an interaction. What could you have done differently? Why?

* 60-DAY OPTION *

Tomorrow, apply what you can do differently and consider someone else's values more than your own.

day | ten

a | different | vantage | point

"It is nice to be around people who think differently than you. They challenge your ideas and keep you from being complacent."

– Tucker Carlson

remember one Good Friday when I actually took a day off. Most of my clients were closed, so I chose to spend the day with my youngest daughter. We went into the city to see a fun and interesting "Big Apple Circus" for the day. While we could have easily driven, my daughter really wanted to take the train into the city, so we boarded in our local town. I have taken the train many, many times but it is different when you're looking out the window with a seven-year-old. I saw things I typically don't notice.

I noticed how very different the same old things looked to me when I viewed them through the window of the train. There are certain towns we go through, industrial parks where I visit clients, stores where I shop, etc. that looked so unusual to me when I was sailing past them in a train. I found it hard to get my bearings.

The experience reminded me how hard it can be to step outside of our everyday built-in filters when we are trying to understand others, or work and live with them more effectively. We want to be open-minded and come at a relationship or situation a different way, but in too many cases we end up so far outside of our comfort zone that we go back to looking through the lens that feels most natural to us.

Here's a personal example: When my teenage daughter acts like a teenager, I imagine her to be the little girl who wrote me love notes and told me I was the "best mommy ever." As she yells at me for some real or imagined misdeed, I actually see her with her pigtails and her sweet younger face. This new filter allows me to approach her differently and refrain from yelling back or becoming defensive.

With my clients, when I feel I am not getting through or find myself frustrated by a lack of progress, I imagine the situation to be working well and for us to be finding joint solutions. It helps me to get unstuck from an endless loop and start to think about possibilities.

Am I deluding myself? In some ways, yes. You might be thinking that my idea of a "filter" is actually a simple pair of rose-colored glasses. But here's the thing—I am choosing to put a different frame around a situation. I am choosing to think that something COULD be different. Pretending allows me to open my mind to other possibilities and see people through a different lens. It doesn't always magically change what's happening, but it gives me more choices in how I can deal with the person involved. I am able to get unstuck by taking this different viewpoint.

* EXERCISES *

Today, try stepping outside of your comfort zone with someone who pushes your buttons. Try imagining them to be a more positive force in your life, at work, or in some other aspect. You may find you learn something about that other person—and, maybe more importantly, about yourself too!

Put on your rose-colored glasses and take a gander at how the world looks. There's no harm in using a little bit of imagination to help you wade through a difficult situation. Life is hard, why make it any harder? If it helps to put those glasses on for just a minute, do it!

Write about a situation during which you encountered a difficult situation that you interpreted in the same way you always do. What could you have done differently? Why?

* 60-DAY OPTION *

Tomorrow, apply what you can do differently. Put on a pair of rose-colored glasses just long enough to get you through a difficult situation.

day | eleven

you | talk | ing | to | me | ?

"What you do speaks so loud that I cannot
hear what you say."

– Ralph Waldo Emerson

The other day I was having a conversation with my son about his grades. His report card was excellent and he had lower grades in only two classes—Math and Health. I was curious about the health grade—it seems like an easy class, so I wondered out loud why he was not doing better. He said, "Mom, all they teach us in health is what you tell us all the time anyway. I call it the 'Mom class' because it is just your words over and over about taking care of ourselves. And we have these units on bullying—three years now and what difference does it make, kids still bully and the rest of us get sick of listening!"

I thought about how this perspective—having information given over and over to a broad group hoping to capture the minority (in this case, the bullies) but not having human behavior actually change as a result—mimics what I observe in corporate America all the time. I see a company where there are a few people who are doing something "wrong"—it could be coming in late, it could be bad-mouthing the firm, it could be taking long breaks, but whatever it is, management wants to fix it. However, instead of addressing the people involved directly, management will call a meeting and give a "Let's set the record straight" talk. What happens? The people who were already doing things the proper way (like the kids who would never think of bullying) are the only ones listening. The guilty parties don't even know that the message is intended for their ears!

In the corporate world, some people become frustrated because someone on the other side of a dynamic doesn't recognize the role they play in a situation. We all do this at times. For instance, when I get into a debate with my teenager, I want to believe that I am just playing "good mom" and she is the problem — but when I can step outside and be honest, I see that I often exacerbate the situation because of my unwillingness to see the world from her viewpoint. I want what I want in the moment, and considering why she wants something else can be challenging.

So it isn't easy for us to hear a message if we aren't ready, willing, and in a position to do so. Think about the wasted time and energy in schools and in businesses because of this global "just get the message out there" approach. If we examine this method of giving information, it's easy to see that we are wasting time and opportunity talking to people who already "get it" in the hope that we will capture someone who doesn't. Wouldn't that time be better spent targeting specific individuals and performing an intervention with someone or some group directly, instead of beating around the bush?

Many people prefer to avoid a direct approach in order to avoid alienating the guilty. School administrators believe that all of the kids need to hear the message so they can be part of the solution. But is this really working? Are we seeing a behavior change as a result of this approach? I think my son's observation may be on target — the kids are hearing the message, but nothing is changing in their day-to-day life, and they're getting tired of listening. In the business world, people will continue to voice their frustration at management's unwillingness to tackle a problem head-on because the guilty parties don't seem to know it is them and don't seem to make any behavior change as a result.

The problem with the blanket approach is that it doesn't make a problem go away! We frustrate the people who aren't at fault by continuing to talk to them as if they are, and we don't get through to the people who need to hear the message because they're not paying attention.

Honest, direct, and negative feedback is very difficult for most of us to give — and to get.

In the emotional dance I do with my daughter, I don't want to acknowledge sometimes that my approach isn't helping and is potentially hurting the situation. I'd rather be the one telling HER to improve and going along my merry way. This realization helps me to understand how hard it can be if we just aren't ready or able to hear that we need to change. I believe that, in general, most of us need more training on how to recognize behavior in need of correction, and we need to teach those in a "teaching" or managing position how to give feedback in a more direct and helpful way. In many cases, an offender doesn't even know they are at fault.

There are lots of reasons why an offender offends, but if those in charge want to bring about a behavior change, instead of just feeling they have conveyed the message and can move on, it's critical to isolate those at fault, speak with them directly, and find ways to solve the problem where it actually lives. It's not easy, but I believe it is a shift that needs to happen if we ever want to see true behavior change with impact.

* EXERCISES *

Today, practice constructive criticism. Instead of allowing yourself to be frustrated by someone else's behavior, take a look at whether or not you have clearly defined your expectations. Don't just assume someone is listening; direct your message to the appropriate person or people.

As we learn to communicate effectively, we also learn that it's terribly unfair to expect others to automatically know what we want or need. Have you ever gotten mad at your spouse because s/he didn't know you didn't like a certain type of music? Have you ever received an attitude from your teenager that you didn't understand? And have you ever gotten frustrated because your coworkers didn't get that you were having a rough day? When your interactions are influenced by you, you may need to explain why; don't just assume that everyone around you automatically knows that you are tired, hungry, frustrated, etc. — tell them!

Write about a situation during which you expected someone or some people to automatically know what you meant or what you needed. What could you have done differently? Why?

* 60-DAY OPTION *

Tomorrow, apply what you can do differently and assume that the people around you are not mind readers. Tell the people around you what you need; don't make them guess.

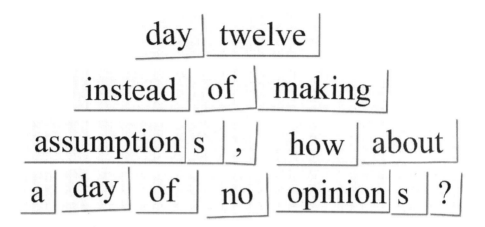

day | twelve

instead | of | making

assumption | s | , | how | about

a | day | of | no | opinion | s | ?

"We are all inclined to judge ourselves
by our ideals; others by their acts."

– Harold Nicolson

It's hard not to notice how everyone, from young children to older adults, has an opinion about what someone else should — or should not — be doing: "She shouldn't wear that outfit." "He must be crazy to have that job." "They don't care about their house at all — look at that lawn!"

As I listen to these kinds of comments, I just can't help but think "So what?" I mean really, what difference does it make to my life, or my family, or anything that I care about what someone else does in their lives? Of course these were just small incidents; I haven't been privy to conversations between people engaging in political or religious discussions (maybe people just don't have those around me anymore!) so I'm not even addressing the BIG judgments and disagreements with others that people have. But still, on any given day, we have some sort of reaction to what another person chooses to do in their own life.

Let's think about that for a minute. What kind of world might this be if we didn't feel like we had to have a running commentary — either to ourselves or others — about what someone else is choosing, doing, or being in their own lives? How much more energy might we have to focus on things we do care about?

I can honestly say that I just don't understand why people are so interested in others' lives. I do care a lot about people—and have been called "nosy" by my only sibling more than once because I like to ask questions and learn about others. I'm not trying to form an opinion about what people do—I just want to learn more about them.

I guess maybe I steer clear of judging what other people do because of my desire to keep others from having an opinion about what I do. It's always been hurtful to me to hear someone say something negative about me when that person really doesn't have all of the information they need to form a solid opinion.

That's the rub for me: How many times do we make assumptions and form an opinion about someone without really knowing what it is like to be in their shoes? Sure, we think we know; we know what we see, but we don't really know enough to proffer a judgment one way or the other—we can't.

See if you can catch yourself making comments to yourself about what other people do. We usually think in terms of "like" and "dislike." We see someone's behavior or choices and say "That's good" or "That's bad." What we think is "good" is not always perceived as good by everyone. We each have our own definitions, and we apply them to others fairly regularly.

* EXERCISES *

Today, instead of offering silent, or spoken, opinions about someone else, spend that energy examining your own behavior and interactions. See if you begin to view things a bit differently.

We're all entitled to our own opinions, and try as we may, so many of us unintentionally focus on the flaws of others in order to boost our own morale. The problem is that we are often guilty of those exact same flaws. When you critique someone else's lawn, do you do so from the position of always having a perfect lawn yourself? Really? You've never let your own lawn go for even a day or two? You've never walked out of the house looking like you just crawled out of bed? Did you get "caught"? Did you wonder what that person must think of you? Chances are that people are thinking the same things about you that you think about them.

Write about a situation during which you made an assumption that was based on no information. What could you have done differently? Why?

* 60-DAY OPTION *

Tomorrow, apply what you can do differently and refrain from forming an opinion until you have all the information.

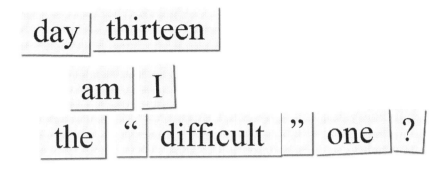

day | thirteen

am | I
the | " | difficult | " | one | ?

> "I learn to see things from different perspectives
> and listen with different ears. The most important
> thing that you need to do is really listen."
>
> – Itzhak Perlman

I once developed and taught a graduate class called "Dealing with Difficult People." Predictably, every participant came in looking for the "secret" to turn that difficult person into someone they want to deal with! I love it when the students had their "ah-ha!" experience and realized that maybe being viewed as difficult is not entirely the other person's fault. In reality, we each have our ways of making things more difficult for ourselves and for others.

If we are honest about our own style and approach, we'll admit that what we do and the way we do it works just fine for us. We get what we want, or we achieve something, and we think "I like my style!" But when we run into those difficult people or difficult situations out there that create trouble for us and wreak havoc with our emotions and reactions, why are we so quick to point the finger and say, "That other person is the problem"? Why don't we immediately say, "How is my style hurting me in this exchange?"

The real difficulty comes when my approach and what I care about collides with you — with your different approach, behavior, and style.

Rather than looking for ways to understand why your actions set me off, or looking at ways that I may be creating difficulty, I assume you are the problem. You are doing something that rocks my boat, and I want you to stop so the waters get calm again for me. My perspective doesn't take you, your needs, or your desires into consideration.

The irony is that, as much as others are a problem for us, for others WE are the problem. When things don't go according to our plan, we get stressed, behave badly, say things we shouldn't, and engage in unproductive relationship behavior. There are many times in any given situation where if we were able to get outside of ourselves and see what we were doing, we would point a finger in the mirror at ourselves and say, "YOU are the difficult one!" But we rarely do this, because it is just easier for us to find fault somewhere, and with someone, else.

Now, I'm not an advocate of mercilessly beating up on oneself. That doesn't help, and it isn't useful for anyone. It's just that, if we operate with more awareness, it becomes easier to see where we can make changes in our own behavior and choose in favor of collaboration instead of divisiveness.

* EXERCISES *

Today, take someone else into consideration. Set what you want aside and put someone else first.

It's hard to believe that we, ourselves, may be viewed as "difficult." After all, it's everyone else that refuses to cooperate. But honestly, think about it; there are two sides to every interaction, and even though s/he may not say so, the person you are interacting with may think you are the problem, just as you are thinking s/he is the problem. Most of us are not immune to the feeling that someone is pacifying us. We also usually realize that that individual is doing so to make a situation easier—probably for everyone involved. So, instead of ending an interaction with the satisfaction that you have converted someone to your way of thought (which really benefits no one), take the other person's opinion into consideration. You don't have to agree; you just have to listen... and maybe compromise.

Write about a situation during which you expected someone else to just accept your argument for or against something. What could you have done differently? Why?

* 60-DAY OPTION *

Tomorrow, apply what you can do differently to change your style in dealing with other people.

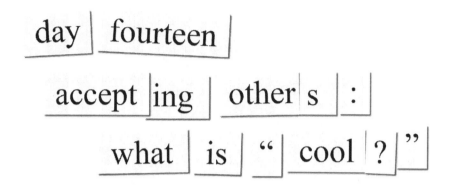

day | fourteen |

accept |ing | other| s | : |

what | is | " | cool |? | " |

> "Consider how hard it is to change yourself and you'll understand what little chance you have in trying to change others."
>
> – Unknown

My son is a very insightful and thoughtful young man. The other day, he informed me that he is "not cool" and therefore could not participate in the talent show event at his elementary school. I asked him how he knew he wasn't "cool." He answered that "everyone knows who is cool and who isn't, Mom."

It's interesting how most of us assume that some people have the option of telling everyone else what's right and what's wrong—and that there is a common definition of which traits are "good" and which are not. When I really pushed my little guy to "define cool," he couldn't do it. He just knows that other kids don't like certain things about him, and he isn't a member of the "in group."

This interaction with my son made me wonder about how most people often just accept what other people think. It's not an uncommon experience, even for adults, to have someone else define "cool" for us. We let others tell us what clothes to wear, what car to drive, what school to send our children to, or what restaurant we choose to dine in on Friday night.

I was struck one day by the conversation between a couple of the moms in my neighborhood as we stood at the school bus stop one day. "Can you believe she chose that color for her new roof? What was she thinking?" asked one. "That's her. She has no taste at all," said the other. I guess the person they were talking about simply did not choose to do what was "cool" and as a result she was (probably unknowingly) ostracized by her neighbors for her lack of foresight.

Interestingly, even if we don't agree with the assertion that something is "uncool," many of us don't contradict the opinion. For instance, when someone is gossiping about someone else, how often have you said, "But I like that person. I don't want to talk about them." If we do choose not to engage in gossip, or if we choose to present an alternative dissenting opinion, then we feel like we aren't "in." And if we aren't "in," then we are not going to be liked. Even as we age, we still want to be the cool ones!

When my daughter was in the fifth grade, and I was volunteering in her class, she begged me to "wear jeans like all of the other moms do" because I often went to her school in my work clothes or wearing my favorite sweatpants. I didn't even own a pair of jeans. It was distressing to me how much she cared about my appearance and how much she needed me to fit in and be "cool." Kids feel the pressure, and that pressure extends to the adults around them.

* EXERCISES *

Today, think about whether you are defining "cool" for someone else. If you are, consider dropping the need to define anything at all — if you can do this, you'll find out what it really means to be "cool!" Also, think about whether you are letting someone else define cool for you. There's nothing wrong with being different.

I'll bet you think pretty highly of your own opinions. After all, they are based on fact and personal experience, right? It's not like you just formed an opinion out of nowhere. But just because your experiences and beliefs have caused you to develop one way of thinking doesn't mean that your opinion makes you an authority on… well… anything. It pays for us all to realize that what is "right" and what is "wrong" is subjective.

Write about a situation during which you passed judgment based on what you believed was "right" or "wrong," "cool" or "uncool." What could you have done differently? Why?

* 60-DAY OPTION *

Tomorrow, apply what you can do differently and look at the actions/decisions of others without adding your own values, preferences, or opinions to the mix. Try to see how refraining from inserting a bit of yourself into someone else's life changes the way you see someone else's behavior or decisions.

week three

don't be the rule - be the exception !

love Christmas music. One of my favorites is a silly song that my youngest child listens to from a Santa cartoon. The song is about a "despicable" guy who is trying to change from bad to good. The little elf who is coaching the guy tells him that "changing from bad to good is as easy as putting one foot in front of the other," and then the elf goes on to sing a great little tune in which he tells the guy "don't be the rule, be the exception!"

Given the work I do, I find myself singing this song at the very top of my lungs. It's such an uplifting idea to me that, as hard as change is for most people, it CAN happen — but often it takes one step at a time. Each day we are all given the chance to do something differently in our interactions with others. It's so easy to fall into the same old patterns, but we can become the exception and try something different each time we choose to.

Change is really about becoming more aware. We have all taken years to develop the approaches we have — whether they serve us or not! Becoming aware of how we react to others is a first step on the road to change.

As many years as I've been doing this work, I will still fall into certain patterns with certain people. It's only after I've acted that I recognize what I've done, and then have to make a choice about what I will do next — one foot in front of the other... Behavior triggers are deeply ingrained, and when we are tired or stressed or otherwise weak in our personal resources, we may find that "changing from bad to good" takes more effort and more energy than we thought. So, instead of setting an unreachable goal, take one little step designed to bring you closer to a new place.

Here's an example: I have had a very difficult time with a particular neighbor. She hates my dogs, but instead of talking to me, she calls the police or walks by me on the street without speaking. I find myself going out of my way to avoid her, rather than dealing with her unpleasant behavior. I was invited to a "ladies luncheon" by another neighbor whom I simply adore. She is one of my favorite people, so I wanted to attend, but the "difficult" neighbor was also going to be there. For me, one foot in front of the other meant going to the luncheon and spending time with someone who has been very hurtful toward me. I had to make a choice to do something I wanted to, in spite of the uncomfortable position it put me in.

Dealing with people who challenge us in one way or another is complex, and it sure isn't always easy. But putting one foot in front of the other means we can't turn away or ignore something just because it makes us uncomfortable. It helps to realize that my difficult neighbor makes me feel guilty because I didn't know she was bothered by my dogs. Understanding that I am not a mind reader, and could never have been expected to know how she felt, allowed me to release myself from that guilt. Recognizing this dynamic gave me the confidence I needed to go into the luncheon and say a cheery "hello" to everyone present—including my difficult neighbor.

As you navigate this week's exercises, think about one step you can take with someone who challenges you, even if the step is just spending some time thinking about the reasons they challenge you. Don't put pressure on yourself to make a wholesale change; just do one thing you might not have done before.

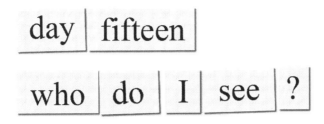

day | fifteen |

who | do | I | see | ? |

"The ability to perceive or think differently is more important than the knowledge gained."

– David Bohm

I love Elton John. I've been listening to his music since I was a kid, and he is still in wonderful form. The words of one of his well-known songs, "Don't Let the Sun Go Down on Me" written by Elton and Bernie Taupin, really struck me as I was singing along one day. There is a line that says "Although I search myself, it's always someone else I see." I started to think about this line in the context of the work I do in helping people to understand others—and themselves.

We tend to put a positive frame around our own actions and reactions. No matter what we do, we often tell ourselves that we "mean well" in our approach. We might color our harsh words, explaining attitude or impatience with "I was trying to do the right thing." But this same behavior, when we notice it in others, can be intolerable to us. There is a line of psychology that talks about the shadow aspect of our personalities. This means that there are parts of our beings that we don't really want to acknowledge, so we keep them in the shadow. But when we observe this same behavior in others, we react very negatively to it. It's as if we don't want to own that this is part of ourselves, so we just push it away.

Listening to Elton sing his famous song, I began to think. I search myself and try to understand myself, but do I accept and believe what I see, or do I push it away and say that it must be someone else who is doing the things I don't like to believe I am also capable of doing? We may have one image of ourselves as a certain kind of person, and any kind of information or insight that says we are really a different kind of person is bound to upset us.

Think about a time you were "accused" of some behavior or some approach, and you felt you were wrongly accused. Once, when my son was talking to me, I was admittedly not paying enough attention. He asked me a question, and I couldn't respond. He cried out to me, "Mom—you never listen to what I say, and you aren't listening now." Instead of admitting my guilt, I tried to tell him all of the times that I do listen and how, of course, I'm interested in what he has to say.

But, truth be told (and as I did tell him a few minutes later), I was not listening to him in that moment. Instead of just admitting that, I became defensive. It's true, there are times that I am preoccupied, and I am just not paying attention. I can make many excuses for why this is, but the excuses don't matter. What matters is that I have to "own" my behavior even if I don't like it.

Truly seeing what we do and how we act can be a wonderful learning experience. We each need to search for and embrace all of what we see—the good, the bad, and the ugly! If we push it away, or believe it isn't a part of who we are, we actually limit our chances of changing and growing and becoming better people in our relationships.

When we search ourselves, we have to want to see the parts that we don't love, and we can't embrace. These are the parts that will prove to be our teachers over time and will help us to have more compassion toward others who may have these traits, too.

* EXERCISES *

Today, make a commitment—before the sun goes down on you—to open your eyes and embrace all of who you are. Don't like what you see? Stare it in the face and take steps to change.

Think you're perfect? Well, don't we all! At least, pretty darned close. All joking aside, there isn't (or shouldn't be) one of us who truly believes s/he is perfect. Honestly, life would be pretty boring if we were perfect. In lieu of perfection, it sure behooves most of us to at least attempt to be the person we'd like others to believe we are. But you know what? That's hard to do!

It's a lot easier to excuse away imperfection than it is to be the person we want others to see. There's no way you're going to be perfect, but you sure can work toward searching yourself and truly liking what you see.

Write about how you want others to see you. What characteristics are important to you? What can you do to be that person?

* 60-DAY OPTION *

Tomorrow, work on being the person you want others to see. Pick one characteristic—more if you're energetic—and work on making a change to truly become that person. No excuses!

day | sixteen

guilty | by | association

"People don't change their behavior unless it
makes a difference for them to do so."

– Sharon Stone

I recently read a disturbing report about how immigrant children come
to this country relatively lacking in violence and bullying behavior.
However, the longer they reside in the U.S., the higher the rate of violence and bullying they exhibit. Experts in the school systems interviewed
for the article said that this news is "not surprising" to them.

Not surprising?! Really?! It's not surprising that we have created a culture where instead of learning kindness and compassion and how to look
out for one another, we have taken someone who was not formerly prone
to violence and forced them to become violent by associating with our
school children?!

I would hope this would be surprising. The fact that it isn't, reflects a sad
picture of our current thinking. To survive in many of our city schools,
kids need to be violent and angry so that they can protect themselves from
others who would want to hurt them.

I think we need to ask what's happening to our children that bullying is a preferred state. Instead of moving to a new country and feeling
embraced, children feel as though they have to assert their own strength

to avoid being the subject of bullying and ridicule. I firmly believe that people lash out at others because they are missing a foundational sense of "I'm okay" deep down inside. Rather than feeling unconditional love from their parents or their teachers, kids are forced to erect a wall of protection so that they can't be hurt.

It's not just in our cities, of course. Sometimes the stories I hear from my own children about how they are spoken to by teachers or other school leaders are appalling to me. The sarcasm or anger the teachers display toward the children they teach provides a negative role model. My kids come home and talk to me about it, but many kids do not utter a word; they suffer in silence. Or, even worse, when they do come home and report the abuse, they are also verbally bullied by their own parents.

"Kill or be killed" seems to be the emotional mantra that many of our children practice. Instead of looking at life as "We're all in this together — let's make the best of it," interactions become about "who can I lash out at today to secure my spot as the strongest bully around." Immigrant children, according to the study, watch this and decide that if they are going to fit in and have friends, they'd best follow suit.

As adults, we need to look at the role model we are providing for our children. How tolerant are we of others' differences? How quick are we to judge or criticize another person? How quickly do we lash out at someone instead of trying to understand them?

* EXERCISES *

Today, take note of your responses to others. The goal is not to judge yourself or criticize your own behavior, but rather to learn about the image you portray to anyone—child or adult—who may be watching you and learning. If people around you are to be "guilty by association," what kind of behavior do you want them to display?

Do you bring your best to the table during every interaction? Probably not. After all, we all experience stress, a bad day, fatigue, and many, many other factors that negatively influence behavior. But you don't have to let external factors affect the way you present yourself. Someone is always watching; make every interaction count.

Write about a situation during which you didn't act in a way that would present you as a positive role model (nor just for your kids, but for anyone—coworkers, neighbors, family members, etc.). What could you have done differently? Why?

* 60-DAY OPTION *

Tomorrow, apply what you can do differently and become a role model.

day | seventeen

motivating | through | caring

> "I have found that the more we care for the happiness of others, the greater is our own sense of well-being."
>
> – The Dalai Lama

The January/February 2011 issue of *Sales Power* magazine has an article where I am interviewed on being a "model manager." The lead-in to the article states that "you can only evolve people one at a time." This was such a great opportunity for me — to be interviewed by Kim Wiley on this topic. I think in sales, as in many areas of life, we treat people as if they were dollar signs, a means to an end, and not as human beings.

Is it just easier for a company to define employees as "they" instead of as individual people? Admittedly, it takes time on the part of a manager to learn something about each staff member and to understand what it takes to motivate each individual. The managers who do take the time to do this are often rewarded with insights into motivating behaviors. They are also often rewarded with loyalty. After all, who doesn't feel good when someone has taken the time to know them and to care about them?

I often liken management to parenting. It would be a luxury to just say, "Do it!" and expect you will be blindly followed and obeyed. In many cases, parents and managers do this and they are followed — but often not by loyalists who willingly do what is required. Rather, the person who issues commands about what needs to be done may get what they want, but they lose respect and loyalty in the process!

If you are in a position of management or control in an organization, you have to ask yourself what you really want to accomplish. In many companies, the profit line is the only thing that management cares about. But with all of our advancements in technology and computing, people continue to be the backbone of almost every organization. People are the key to a healthy bottom line. If people are not motivated and excited about what they do, or at a minimum trained and heard, they can't possibly operate at a productive level of effectiveness.

It's an interesting quandary for managers. People who feel good about what they do, and are intrinsically motivated to succeed, will often go the extra mile and do more than is requested of them. So a manager that focuses solely on profit and has no regard for people will actually reduce profit because they are getting less out of their people than they could if they were more focused on the employees! What does this mean? It means that taking care of people and having compassion and interest is actually economically beneficial for most companies. Seems counterintuitive, right? If you spend time coddling your staff, you won't get anything done! But in fact the opposite is true; if you get to know the people who work for you, understand their obstacles, and do your best every day to remove those obstacles, you can create a better-functioning, well-oiled machine that will help you achieve the profit levels you desire.

In my consulting work I am often in a position to talk to people very intimately about what they deal with on a day-to-day basis. It's surprising to me how little the people in charge know about what goes on "down in the trenches" of their firm. This not knowing can be perilous because, in many cases, employees have information that the managers really need—but if a manager doesn't ask for it, or doesn't send the message that they are open to listening, that information will stay locked down in the troops. It may surface at some point as a problem for management, and many, many times I hear management say, "Why didn't anyone tell me this?" My answer? "Because you weren't listening."

* EXERCISES *

Today, take the time to know your people, to care about what they are dealing with, and to address their problems—in their personal life and in business. When you do this, you'll find that you actually reduce the amount of problems you are dealing with, and you get more—and more effective—behavior!

Decades ago, the workplace functioned as a mini kingdom. Employees were serfs and management was royalty. Although there is certainly still a hierarchy we have to respect at work, studies have consistently shown that happy workers are productive workers. That means it is a good idea for all of us to get to know the "little people" at work.

Write about a situation during which you didn't treat someone "below" you at work with the respect they deserve. What could you have done differently? Why?

* 60-DAY OPTION *

Tomorrow, apply what you can do differently to make sure that you, and those you work with, respect each other.

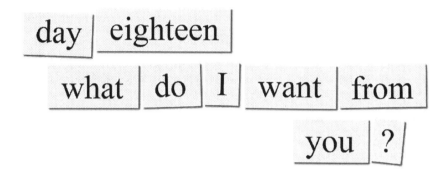

day | eighteen

what | do | I | want | from

you | ?

"I must respect the opinions of others even if I
disagree with them."

– Herbert Henry Lehman

During a recent radio show interview, I had the pleasure of talking about many things related to the general lack of civility in some discussions in the public arena. I heard from callers from all over the world, asking questions and sharing viewpoints. I enjoyed the dialogue immensely.

One caller asked my perspective on a disagreement he was having with a friend of his on the issue of gun control. The caller gave his position and basically went on to say that his friend was not willing to listen to, or understand, another viewpoint. As he talked, I began to understand that neither the caller nor his friend would be able to convince the other of a different opinion. The caller wanted to know what I thought about his friend who refused to listen.

Have you ever wondered why another person is so unwilling to see your way of thinking? We all have very strong opinions on certain topics. Learning to respect other people and other viewpoints doesn't mean we agree with everything we hear. We may have an emotional attachment to a certain topic that is very meaningful to us. But is it really a good idea to spend a lot of energy arguing with someone who fundamentally disagrees with us, expecting that person to change his mind?

Think of the wasted energy that is expended during a disagreement between two people who both realize that they will never agree. What can be gained by continuing to do verbal battle with someone who has a different perspective, a different set of values, and a very different filter on the world (or on the topic at hand) from our own?

This is not to say that we shouldn't voice an opinion. Change happens on many fronts because there is a place for education and debate. New information comes to light, and many people who may have believed one thing may find a new perspective. The problem is with the manner in which people tend to engage in these disagreements.

Look at it this way: I set out to convince you that your viewpoint is wrong and mine is right. Most times we aren't even listening to one another; we are just listening for a "cue" to give us another chance to present our case. Is this productive and conducive to building relationships and common ground between us? In most cases, it's not.

When people are passionate about something, it's hard to see any other perspective. It's almost as if another perspective just doesn't exist—or shouldn't exist. We hear someone voice something counter to our own thinking, something is triggered, and we react. And, depending on the depth of our feelings about the issue, we don't usually stick to the data and facts—we make it very personal about the other person. "How could YOU be a person who believes X?" "You are one of THEM?"

Have you ever worked with someone, or known someone, and you liked the person, but then you learned that they subscribed to a certain viewpoint or position on a subject and all of a sudden your perspective on that person changed? In reality, the person didn't change, and the part you liked was still there, but the values they expressed colored your viewpoint of who they really were.

In our culture there are many ways to express our opinions. We can blog, we can write an editorial, we can vote, we can speak at a local town meeting, we can contribute to a charity that is working toward the change we want, we can hold forums to educate others, etc., etc. But many, many people don't choose to productively work for the change they want; they spend their time and their energy complaining to and about others. It's neither beneficial nor useful, and it definitely creates rifts in relationships. It's so much easier for me to demonize you if I believe your views are "wrong."

* EXERCISES *

Today, work for change in yourself and in others by accepting that everyone is entitled to his or her own opinion and that those opinions may differ from yours. Pick one person's opinion—at work, at home, or in the media—and spend a little time exploring that opinion in a more open-minded and deliberate manner. When all is said and done, you may still disagree, but at least you learned something.

Most of us are guilty of forcing our opinions on others at some time or another. Sometimes we don't even realize we are doing it. Have you ever become frustrated because your teenager didn't understand why you were less than fond of her boyfriend? Have you ever been guilty of forming an immediate opinion of someone because of the way they looked? Things like behavior, race, gender, religion, etc. give us ways to identify people, but many of us take it too far and use those qualities to categorize others.

Write about a situation during which you categorized someone because of the way they looked, acted, or believed. What could you have done differently? Why?

* 60-DAY OPTION *

Tomorrow, apply what you can do differently to avoid categorizing someone. Listen to others and interact based on what you hear, not what you assume.

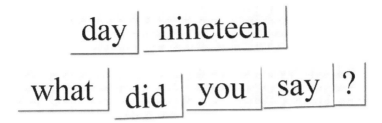

day | nineteen

what | did | you | say | ?

"We have two ears and one mouth so that we can listen twice as much as we speak."

– Epictetus

I was once asked by a member of a state government if I would be willing to speak to a group of employees. I posted a note about this invitation on my Facebook page, and commented about how difficult it seems to be to work in state government these days. That post received a comment from someone who went on and on about the health laws in Arizona. Huh? I had to read the response several times to make sure I understood it, as it was a complete *non sequitur* to my post about state government.

A couple of my friends called me to remark on how odd the response was relative to what I had written. My first reaction was to respond and point out to the person who commented that they really didn't read what I was writing—and didn't respond to the actual issue I had posted about. But then I stopped and looked at the situation from a different angle.

I could clearly see how this person's filters (filters are the invisible film that sits between our understanding and the other people out there in the world we are interacting with on a daily basis) colored his or her experiences.

Filters "color" our experience because, instead of seeing clearly what's happening, we see everything as it's delivered to us through our filters. So, if my filter is that the laws in Arizona vis-à-vis healthcare are bad, I will find opportunities via what others say to affirm this — like the person on my Facebook page. Filters certainly aren't limited to political viewpoints, though. They color most issues we encounter with others. We often don't "see" the person or issue in front of us because all we can "see" is our expectation of them, or our own experiences.

Have you been in a situation where you are trying to be really clear with someone about something important to you — you are doing your best to explain your position and your thinking — but the other person simply isn't hearing you? That's because the other person is likely responding to something that has been colored by his or her own filters — not the reality of the interaction. Interactions like this can be very frustrating because it's easy to believe that the other person doesn't care or is focused on something else. In fact, they ARE focused on something else — but even they may not be aware of it.

Filters can lead us into all kinds of difficulty with others. We may not give someone the opportunity to explain themselves if we respond too quickly to what has been said. We may find ourselves in a fight with someone and end up needing to swallow our pride, when we realize we didn't fully understand what the other person was saying before we opened our own mouth to respond.

Filters are a fact of life. While we think we are honest and fair in our interactions with others, the truth is that our filters color everything we see and hear. We perceive others in relation to our expectations. We often just react — and don't even know why we are reacting. Like the person on my Facebook page, we may present a response to someone and leave them wondering, "Did they even listen to anything that I said?" If we find ourselves feeling misunderstood, sometimes we just shut down and don't bother even trying to communicate!

The only way to really deal with the filters is to put your energy into active listening and focusing on other people. Check for understanding in your interactions and ensure that what someone said is what you actually heard. Before you react, give yourself some time to digest what's been said and observe your own reaction to it.

Many relationships have been ruined by a misunderstanding. Be sure you are seeing clearly in your relationships, in order to give others the best opportunity to be heard and understood.

* EXERCISES *

Today, work on your personal filters. Really listen to what someone else is saying. Don't assume that you know where that person is coming from without asking. Clarify everything. Try repeating what the person said, to reinforce the interaction and show that you are really listening.

We've all been guilty of reacting in a way that is unrelated to the situation at hand. Others may be able to see that our actions are not based on what is going on, but we may be so caught up in our own little world that we don't see what others do. Later, after we've had a chance to look at the situation, we often see just where we went wrong. Make sure that you, in every interaction, attend to the matter at hand and not to what you think is going on.

Write about a situation during which you let your personal filters color an interaction. What could you have done differently? Why?

* 60-DAY OPTION *

Tomorrow, apply what you can do differently to avoid letting your filters get in the way of understanding others.

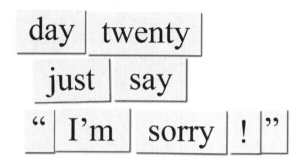

day | twenty

just | say

" | I'm | sorry | ! | "

> "Every time we start thinking we're the center of the universe, the universe turns around and says with a slightly distracted air, 'I'm sorry. What'd you say your name was again?'"
>
> – Margaret Maron

Recently, I was reminded of how difficult it can be to remain impartial and refrain from reacting when someone else is really doing something that feels offensive—especially if that person just refuses to apologize.

I was once at a baseball game when my 12-year-old son was playing. It was an important game for him, because a win or a loss meant the difference between ending the season in 2nd or in 3rd place. The team was playing very well, and my son was having one of his best games ever. There was a young man umpiring behind the plate. He clearly had not been schooled on the rules, because he kept making very bad calls. In three cases, his calls led to the opposing team getting a run that they never should have gotten. The situation became so extreme that even my son's level-headed, calm coach was boiling over with frustration.

I was watching the umpire and his actions and reactions. He seemed like he didn't even care that his calls were bad and the team was devastated. My son came over to the fence where I was watching and said, "Mom—I don't mind if we play badly and lose, but it stinks if we lose because this guy is so wrong!"

When I saw the umpire in the parking lot later on, he was on his cell phone and clearly upset. I'm sure being in the hot seat wasn't much fun for him, either. When my son came out and got into the car with me, he was very frustrated. "If only he had said 'I'm sorry,' Mom," he said to me, "it would've made it better, but he pretended like nothing was wrong."

That vignette summed up two of the most powerful words in the universe: "I'm sorry." When someone does something to us that is upsetting, whether they mean to or not, it hurts. It seems that it hurts so much more, though, when the other person just won't admit they are sorry. But, as we all know by now, we can't get other people to do what we want them to—we can only control our own actions.

The worst four-letter word in the dictionary is the adjective "fair," because, in reality, there is no such thing. I wanted my son to understand that life isn't fair, but we don't want to use this as an excuse to devolve into being a hating and unhappy human being. We have to shake it off and move on.

The other thing we talked about was the importance of admitting when you're wrong and taking responsibility for your behavior. It doesn't feel good to say "I made a mistake," but when we do, we reach a deeper level in our relationship with others because we are able to humble ourselves to another person. If that person is important to us, offering the olive branch and admitting our own human frailties can be very freeing and offer us release. Holding on to hurt knowing that we've hurt someone else is never good for anyone.

* EXERCISES *

Today, think about someone to whom you can extend an olive branch—perhaps someone you have had difficulty with and you've allowed a chasm to grow between you. Be the one to offer the branch. The other person may not accept it, but it's important to make the effort anyway.

There's no doubt that saying you're sorry for something is hard. Sometimes we refuse to apologize because we just don't believe we're at fault. Occasionally, an apology isn't warranted because we're "wrong," but because we didn't give someone else full credit or acknowledgement for their feelings, position, etc. Apologies are also difficult because overusing them can negate them. It's important to be sincere when apologizing, even when you aren't convinced you're in the wrong.

Write about a situation during which an apology was warranted but you didn't offer one. Why not? What could you have done differently? Why?

* 60-DAY OPTION *

Tomorrow, apply what you can do differently to reach out and apologize to someone.

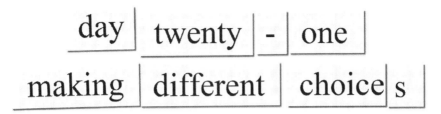

day twenty - one
making different choices

> "Take the trouble to stop and think of the other person's feelings, his viewpoints, his desires and needs. Think more of what the other fellow wants, and how he must feel."
>
> – Maxwell Maltz

Many people who have read my book *Understanding Other People: The Five Secrets to Human Behavior* tell me that they had an "ah-ha" moment when they realized that other people are not necessarily "difficult"—they are not deliberately trying to drive them crazy!

When we take an objective look at what others are doing and saying, and we refuse to impulsively "judge" or to react, we often find that others are not trying to annoy us, but rather they are simply hurting human beings.

Most parents are familiar with a cranky child that refuses to politely ask, "Can you help me?" Instead, the crankypuss would rather whine, cry, and throw tantrums, seeking the support that they need. Bad behavior doesn't benefit them, but it does generate a response from the adult in charge.

We grown-ups are not so different from cranky children. Sometimes we don't have the words we need or the peace inside to calmly ask for what we want. We get angry, frustrated, or depressed because we can't give voice to our real needs. Many times we aren't even sure what we need—we just know we aren't getting it!

When we lash out at others, or become otherwise difficult in our relationships, we are causing pain to ourselves and to others. Instead of being a person who reacts and then feels badly for the way they treated someone, practice being the person that says "Instead of letting another person 'trigger' me and allowing myself to respond with a knee-jerk reaction, I will pause and be watchful about what's happening in the exchange. I will give myself the critical few seconds to step outside of the communication and be aware of the other person and of my own reactions."

Taking the time to assume this position won't make the other person behave differently toward you, and it might not make the exchange any easier, but it will give you another option in terms of how you choose to respond.

Most of the time we respond without even realizing what we're doing, and then we wish we could take it all back and start over.

* EXERCISES *

Today, practice starting over before you begin. Allow yourself the few seconds needed to calmly look over your interactions, develop a number of possible responses, and then choose the one that actually meets your needs.

Use your big boy/girl words to express how you feel, rather than lashing out at someone. Take a breath, count to ten, or just give yourself a few moments to think before you respond or react.

Write about a situation during which you reacted without thinking. What could you have done differently? Why?

* 60-DAY OPTION *

Tomorrow, apply what you can do differently to avoid letting a situation get out of control.

week four

reframing bad behavior

've learned many useful things over the years through my hypnosis training, but one thing that has stood out for me has been the idea of "reframing." Reframing is an NLP (neuro-linguistic programming) technique that can be a very powerful tool to help you move from stuck to unstuck, and to give you more energy to deal with things that frustrate you.

Let's face it, as much as we may understand about others and about our own reactions to people, there will always be people that bug us. I'm often asked if learning about this work means no more difficult people, and the answer is "of course not!" As many times as I step outside to observe and refrain from reacting, there are just as many times that I let my emotions and labels get the better of me, and I find myself running away with my own frustrations.

The process of reframing is a great way to switch gears when you find yourself unable to "STOP!" Reframing goes like this: When I see a situation that is bothersome to me, I somehow frame or label that situation in a different way. For example, one weekend I was at a water park with my children. There was a man sitting at the only available picnic table—one man. This table could have held about five people, and this one man was holding it—presumably for his family to show up at some point. There was a woman with four children, all holding hot food and eyeing his table. She said, "Couldn't we just sit there until your party comes?" and he answered, quite gruffly, "No—I got here first!" The woman and her children then had to sit on the concrete floor to eat their lunch. I was sitting at a bar table nearby watching this—my family was all in the water having fun at the time. The woman next to me saw me watching and said,

"What a jerk, huh? Nothing like being mean to a bunch of little kids! If I were that woman, I would've given him a piece of my mind!"

As I sat there, I could feel myself beginning to agree with this woman that this man was a jerk. But then I considered the opportunity to reframe. What if this guy had problems of his own? What if he had a handicapped child coming? What if he was just a fearful, protective person who had experienced some bad things in life and was reacting as a result? What if he had some other considerations or issues that the rest of us knew absolutely nothing about? The truth is that there were many tables in this park with other people sitting at them; he just happened to have the one that was seemingly empty. By reframing, I tried to put a frame around him and be compassionate toward him as a troubled person instead of the "jerk" that my seatmate was making him out to be. The truth is that I don't know that man's story and I never will. However, the process of having to practice reframing was helpful to me. How much do we really ever know about another person before we slap on a label and judge them?

The first time I was in a grocery store, after having been laid up for several months from a car accident that almost killed me, I was very wobbly on my feet. The sheer process of walking through the aisles was overwhelming to me, and I found myself needing to stop and pause every few steps. As I was trying to read the signs overhead, a couple came around the corner of the aisle. "Look at this witch," the woman said, "she could care less about anyone else — just standing here blocking the aisle!" It took me a few minutes to figure out she was talking about me, and when I realized it, I moved to the side. I didn't intend to be rude, I was just having a hard time getting my bearings. A few aisles further over, I stopped again and lo and behold, the same couple comes around the corner. "Good Lord! If you could get arrested for rude, this woman would be taken away," she said about me. But was I really being "rude"? In her eyes, yes, but the reframe is that I was trying hard to do a normal life activity that was causing me great difficulty. I learned right there that things aren't always as they seem, and it behooves us to stop and remember that. Reframing someone's bad behavior with a positive possibility can give us freedom to deal more effectively with that person. It might even teach us something about ourselves and someone else.

As you work through the exercises this week and learn how to put everything you've learned into play, find at least one occasion to reframe. As you catch yourself ruminating over someone's bad behavior, just "STOP!" and regroup. Imagine other scenarios that might also fit the circumstances. A colleague of mine says, "If you are going to make something up about someone else, you may as well make up something positive!" So this week, try it and see what happens!

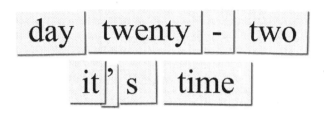

day | twenty | - | two
it's | time

"No one is as deaf as the man who will not listen."

– Jewish Proverb

I remember once working with a hypnosis client who wanted to lose weight. She was a single, working mom and felt she had devoted enough time to everyone else and was ready to devote some time to herself. She expressed her frustration with her own decisions and kept saying she "knew" she should make different choices.

With hypnosis, the important thing is that the person is ready to make a shift—they feel like it is time to cast off whatever has been holding them back and forge ahead into a new area of their lives. Many times, when I meet with people like this client, they almost seem ashamed that they couldn't make the shift on their own without some help.

This is true for any of us who are seeking to be different in our relationships and different in the world in general. Let's face it—the political scene, the news scene, the local store where a manager might be yelling at an employee, or the hockey game where parents are beating up on one another on behalf of their kids don't give us many examples of strong relationships and a show of kindness and compassion for others.

But this doesn't mean we can't wake up each day and say to ourselves,

"It's time." It's time to stop yelling at my significant other and saddling him/her with the responsibility of my unhappiness. It's time to stop blaming my boss or the conditions at work for my bad moods. It's time to stop engaging in the back-and-forth with my teenager that always ends with no solution. It's time to remove people from my life who are not contributing anything positive.

Whatever the situation may be for you, it's time. It won't be easy. No one can say he or she will wake up tomorrow and all will be well. We all have ingrained habits and "triggers" that set us off, and many times, our best intentions go awry because we mean to do something differently but we find ourselves right back where we started, and defeated. "Why bother," many people wonder.

But like my weight loss client, each of us can make a renewed commitment to make different choices. Yes, we used hypnosis to talk to her subconscious mind, but she also had to make some conscious choices to change. She had to take out her calendar and mark the days she would exercise. She had to put the chips that her son enjoys in a cabinet just for him, and put carrots and snap peas in a bowl where she could grab them anytime she needed a snack.

Similarly, we have to figure out what steps we can take to forge deeper relationships. Is the key to listen more effectively? Is it to refrain from cutting someone off while they are talking? Is it to stop turning every conversation we engage in back to ourselves? Maybe it is our behavioral style — do we need to practice more patience in some situations? Do we need to control our anger more effectively?

Identifying where we want to shift and then creating a plan for making the shift can be very effective. It gives us a way to watch what we are doing and also track our progress.

* EXERCISES *

Today, consider making a plan for change. Identify your triggers and see what you can do to put the steps in place to be different.

We've all been guilty of blaming others for our inability to reach a goal. How many times have you heard "I can't lose weight because my husband/wife can eat anything s/he wants" or "I didn't get the promotion because my coworker undermined me" or "I didn't pass the test because the teacher made it too hard." The fact is that no one is responsible for making things happen for you. You have to take the bull by the horns and take control, responsibility, and credit for what you do or don't do.

Write about a situation during which you didn't take responsibility for making a change happen. What could you have done differently? Why?

* 60-DAY OPTION *

Tomorrow, apply what you can do differently to take responsibility, credit, and control to reach a goal.

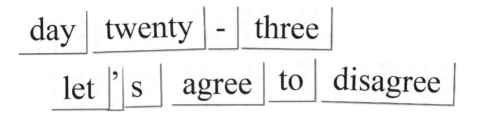

day | twenty | - | three
let | ' | s | agree | to | disagree

> "If we must disagree, let us agree to disagree
> without being disagreeable."
>
> – Unknown

I received an email from a woman who works at a state agency. She had heard me speak on the radio and was intrigued, because in her office people do not get along and it isn't fun for anyone to go to work anymore. As I read her note, I heard the news report about the tragic shooting of Arizona Congresswoman Gabrielle Giffords. An innocent nine-year-old girl was killed during that shooting. She was there to learn more about politics, and she did not live to see another day.

What is it with politics in our country? What is it with the general sense that if I don't agree with you, I simply hate you and you must be banished from my life—and from the Earth? Why is there so much vitriol between people who stand on different sides of the issues?

Personally, I've never been a fan of politics. I am a happily-registered Independent, and I believe the current two-party system is very divisive. My take on politics is a topic for another day, but what I don't understand is why people can't just agree to disagree.

When people disagree, they are generally disagreeing over a viewpoint, a belief, or a value. This is because we all hold different things near and dear. If you and I agree on the same values—and on how to manifest them, or implement the ideas associated with them—all is well. I love someone who sees the world the way I do. But if we disagree, or if my most important values are anathema to you, we may have a very hard time having a civil discussion.

So, if we know this, why can't we just live and let live? I believe it's because people feel triggered by a person or an event and instantly react. Now, thankfully most people don't shoot people they disagree with, but many of us do seethe, avoid, or lash out verbally at others because we don't like what they have to say. Our triggers tell us what to do, instead of our logical mind managing our interactions with others.

It goes like this: We hear or see something we disagree with. We feel attacked, and we take that attack personally. We react. We no longer see the other person as a person with feelings, a heart, and a mind; we just see that individual as "our problem." If we were to see the other person objectively, with our foibles and their foibles intact, we might be able to forge an agreement. Or, at worst, we might agree just to disagree.

I have different values from my husband, from my sister, and from my parents. But I love all of them dearly, so I can be objective about what they care about and why it's different from what I care about. Why am I able to do this with people I love, but not with a congresswoman or someone I hear on television? Because I have something to lose by reacting negatively to the people who are close to me. That barrier isn't there with those we don't know or who are not in our inner circle.

* EXERCISES *

Today, take everyone mentally into your inner circle. If you feel triggered by something someone else says, allow yourself to mentally step outside and see if you can just let it go. Can you agree to disagree instead of being triggered? It's worth a try to attempt to shift the environment you operate in to one more peaceful and accepting of others.

In minor ways, we've all been guilty of condemning someone else because they didn't agree with us. Thank goodness most of us don't overreact to the point where we cause someone else harm, but we do cause sometimes irreparable harm to a relationship — personal or professional — because we are too stubborn to allow others to have a different opinion or belief.

Write about a situation during which you let yourself be triggered by something someone said that you disagreed with. What could you have done differently? Why?

* 60-DAY OPTION *

Tomorrow, apply what you can do differently to allow others to have their opinions and beliefs without sacrificing yours.

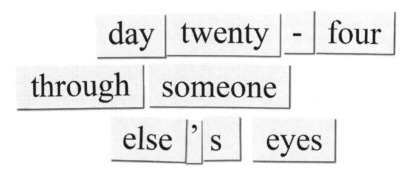

day | twenty | - | four
through | someone
else | ' | s | eyes

"We don't see things as they are,
we see them as we are."

– Anaïs Nin

In my line of work, I often speak to people about a problem or difficulty they are having with someone else. And of course, I'm not immune from my own difficulties with other people. In a recent situation, I had someone who is very close to me send me an angry and disgusted note, saying that I hadn't been a very good friend and hadn't been very responsive to her needs. My first response? "Huh!? Of course I am a good friend and responsive.... Look at what a nice person I am!!"

But when I stepped back a bit, I was able to see the pain that this person was in—a pain actually unrelated to me. This person had depended on me to "fix something" inside of them, but I had failed her. Why? Because this person was waiting for me to act in a certain way. Had I done so, all would have been well with her. Since I didn't act accordingly, she blamed me for her misery.

If only I was different.... Hmmmm, how often does it happen in our daily lives that we believe that if someone else just made a change, did something differently, or was a different kind of person, then WE would be different as a result? Most of us like to think everyone else is the problem, but in fact, everyone else may be waiting for us to make a change too. It's a never-ending cycle of waiting for change.

There have been countless times in my life when I was experiencing problems with someone and was apprehensive about dealing with them, or felt judged or angry by their response to me. In some cases, I had the presence of mind to stop letting the person or situation trigger a reaction and see the other people for who they actually were. In many cases, someone who depends on you to make a change for them is often a scared individual who never learned appropriate coping skills to help them manage their own lives. These little glimpses into the world of others are humbling and elicit compassion—at least they do within me.

People wear masks. Those masks act as filters. Filters are made of experiences. And those filters color everything people see and do. Try to see the person BEHIND the filter in your interactions and conversations. Unfortunately, we can never totally see life through someone else's filter, but we can catch glimpses of the real person behind the mask that each of us wears every day. When we can see the real person, we get a chance to relate as a real person, too. See how many glimpses you can get that might change your view of someone, or give you another way of interacting with them.

* EXERCISES *

Today, as you interact with others, look at yourself and the world around you through someone else's filter. Notice how someone else's experiences make the world a different place.

It isn't easy—many people don't necessarily want you to see their pain, they don't want you to see what hides underneath the filter they have. So to make it easier, you don't have to let anyone know you are doing this. Just practice getting a glimpse whenever you can become conscious enough to do it.

Write about a situation during which you felt that someone wanted you to make things better for them. What could you have done differently? Why?

* 60-DAY OPTION *

Tomorrow, apply what you can do differently to help someone else make a change rather than expecting you to do it for them.

day | twenty | - | five
label s

"Once you label me, you negate me."

– Sören Kierkegaard

A bleeding-heart Liberal." "A Conservative who doesn't care about children." "A tax-and-spend idiot." "A callous person who doesn't want jobs for unemployed people."

With politics becoming more like perpetual campaigns, most of us have become pretty familiar with the comments and barbs being thrown around by our nation's politicians. What's the problem with this? After all, there are two parties that have grown and prospered by throwing these negative monikers at one another and getting people to rally around them.

The problem is that the assumptions we make, the generalizations we apply, and the judgments we assess when someone takes a different position from us are far too often... well... not true. What if we reframed our political discussions to say that "that person is trying to find answers, but I don't agree with the answers they find"? Or even, "that person does care, but I feel like they are misguided in their approach." Wouldn't such an approach be a bit more objective and work to change the way we interact with other people?

I recently ran a workshop at my local chiropractor's office. One woman spoke about a situation with a group she is associated with. She viewed some members of the group as creating some difficulty during the decision-making process. She labeled these people as "catty" or "childish" as a result. After we looked at the situation in some detail, she was able to view her own culpability in her interactions with these folks, and she was able to recognize that they might be merely trying to get some attention or have their views heard. Perhaps the manner in which they chose to get attention was distasteful to her, but their goal was a positive one.

When we use a broad brush to paint people with our judgments and negative words—be it the politician, the person making our lives difficult because of a conflicting style, the sibling who won't return phone calls, the spouse who doesn't do what we'd like—we are reducing our own chances of interacting objectively and productively with those people in our lives. By creating a judgment in response to a behavior we don't like, we actually compromise our own ability to make choices when reacting to someone else. We essentially paint the person and the situation into a box that has no room for objectivity or independence of thought.

I firmly believe that most human beings sincerely try to do their best, but most have limited communication and relationship skills. Most of us don't learn how to be good listeners and to really try to understand what's happening with another person. Our own beliefs, styles, morals, and experiences further compound the communication problem and often prevent us from seeing what's "real."

* EXERCISES *

Today, try to refrain from painting others with the judgment brush. Avoid using terms and labels that are based on judgment. Conversely, pay attention to how other people convey messages colored with their own judgments and labels. We don't have to believe everyone, like everyone, or agree with everyone we encounter, but it is possible to express interest in someone or something without rushing to label it.

We all know that someone who is "difficult" may be hard to deal with. We also know people who are set in their ways. We know, too, that young people don't listen, men don't ask for directions, and women fly off the handle. But what many of us don't know is that people tend to act in ways that we expect them to act. In other words, the way we think someone will behave affects their actual behavior because we guide the interaction down that road. It's important to let all of our interactions unfold in a "pure" way, not colored by our beliefs and judgments.

Write about a situation during which you let a label shade your interaction with someone. What could you have done differently? Why?

* 60-DAY OPTION *

Tomorrow, apply what you can do differently to interact with others based on what you hear from them, not based on the label(s) that may be assigned to them by you or by others.

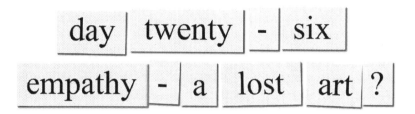

day | twenty | - | six

empathy | - | a | lost | art | ?

"You don't have to accept the invitation to get angry. Instead, practice forgiveness, empathy and encouragement."

– Dan Fallon

An article in my Sunday local paper recently caught me by surprise. It declared that "Empathy is SO yesterday," meaning that young people today don't care much about it. Empathy is something wasted on us old folks, and the kids of today simply don't have the time or inclination to devote any energy to it.

What—no longer a need for empathy? Let's look at the word "empathy." Empathy basically applies to someone who works to understand what another person is feeling or experiencing. When someone is in pain, we empathize with their pain and we feel it too, and we show empathy to that other person.

So the article basically said that the younger people of today no longer feel the need to identify with someone else's thoughts, feelings, or attitudes. Given the interconnectedness of all of us with one another, this seems like a dangerous proposition to me.

Aren't relationships all about trying to understand where someone else is coming from? Isn't the point of interacting to learn what someone else is feeling, thinking, or experiencing, and to try and understand that other person's perspective? If we stop doing this altogether, then aren't we at risk of being completely isolated from every other human being in the world?

We HAVE to care about one another. We have to be interested and put our energy into learning what is really going on with someone else. If we simply don't care, we lose all ability to connect and grow our relationships.

When we don't empathize, and we don't try and understand—that's when it becomes so easy for us to separate ourselves from others and see another person as "a bad guy." This type of disconnect from the people around us can foster bullying or road rage and random acts of anger. If I'm separate from you, and I care nothing about you, I don't have a conscience when it comes to you. Therefore I can depersonalize you and everything associated with you.

Caring, kindness, and empathy are the foundations upon which good relationships are built. The truth is that, at times, we all feel the same kind of pain in life—loneliness, guilt, anger, frustration, hopelessness, or despair. We all feel the same kind of hopefulness that conditions may change, or happiness because of our relationships or something we've done well. Our experiences may be different, but in many ways, everyone's emotional response is the same. By definition, this means that we can understand—and empathize with—one another.

* EXERCISES *

Today, see yourself as part of the larger whole. Work on being someone who watches what happens with others and tries to understand from whence they come. We don't lose anything of ourselves by identifying with another's emotions, but we do gain a much-needed connectedness.

We tend to be a cynical society, and it is that tendency to be cynical that prevents us from true empathy. The fact is that what happens to someone else could easily happen to us, too. For that reason, it's important to let ourselves feel something about the condition of others.

Write about a situation during which you didn't give someone the benefit of your empathy. What could you have done differently? Why?

* 60-DAY OPTION *

Tomorrow, apply what you can do differently to be empathetic. How does empathy make your interactions different?

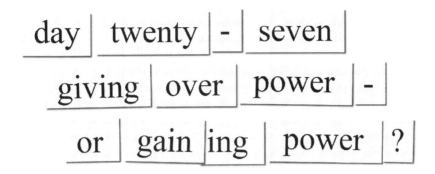

day | twenty | - | seven

giving | over | power | -

or | gain |ing | power | ?

"I am not interested in power for power's sake, but I'm interested in power that is moral, that is right and that is good."

– Martin Luther King Jr.

I once had the pleasure of doing an interview with a wonderful guy for local cable television. My interviewer was very enjoyable, and the hour during which we recorded the interview went by pretty quickly. He brought up a subject that I think is worth addressing.

As a bit of background, I had been interviewed by a local writer for a city paper and we had discussed how frustrating it is when someone cuts in front of you while you're standing in a line. We debated what the proper response to such a slight might be. I shared one of my own experiences when I was with my family and we were "cut" in line by four grown women who actually bragged about cutting. My 11-year-old niece was upset — not only because the four women, supposedly grownups, cut the line, but because they had the insensitivity to brag about their poor behavior. I used the opportunity to teach my kids about rude behavior and how we always have the option to choose our response.

We chose to have a discussion about the people's behavior rather than yell, "Hey — move to the back of the line!" In some other situation, I may have done so but I wanted my kids to learn how to observe difficult behavior without getting emotionally drawn into it.

Some people disagree with this approach. "It isn't good to teach our children to be passive. We need to teach them to stand up for themselves," I've been told. My interviewer that day asked me to respond to the folks that believe we should teach our children to challenge others who don't behave in a socially-acceptable manner. My immediate response to the question was, "Do we?"

Do we need to teach our children that it's never appropriate to just observe someone else behaving badly without jumping in and feeling the need to correct the bad behavior?

Many of us do not realize that, by getting drawn into someone else's bad behavior and giving over our own emotional energy to that person or situation, we actually LOSE our power and control. We have a reduced ability to choose our reaction and fewer options available to us when we immediately feel compelled to jump in and correct another person's behavior.

Stepping outside of a situation and refusing to be drawn in actually gives us more power, more control, and more choices in our lives. We don't "fix" other people by showing them how rude they are—we merely deplete our own energy and release it to someone who doesn't even deserve it! Consider what is happening in the exchange with someone you think of as "rude." You react—you address, or lecture, or yell; they dig in their heels and try to make you the bad guy; you get indignant and yell more; they yell back or make some sarcastic comment, and then what? You both lose.

* EXERCISES *

Today, look for an opportunity to "turn the other cheek." I'm not telling you to let yourself or your rights be trampled on, or to avoid conflict; I'm asking you to choose not to engage with someone who doesn't deserve your engagement. Keep your power and your self-control intact.

YOU have the power to act in any way you deem appropriate. But the fact is that sometimes what seems to be appropriate is not really appropriate. When you take a minute to gauge a situation, you may make a different decision. Sometimes getting involved with someone who behaves badly just isn't worth the effort.

Write about a situation during which you acted aggressively to make a point. What could you have done differently? Why?

* 60-DAY OPTION *

Tomorrow, apply what you can do differently to turn the other cheek. Pick your battles carefully.

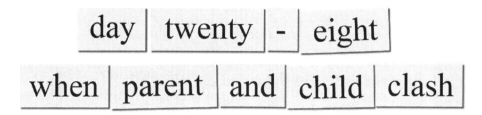

day twenty - eight

when parent and child clash

"When you become defensive, blame others, and do not accept and surrender to the moment, your life meets resistance. Any time you encounter resistance, recognize that if you force the situation, the resistance will only increase. You don't want to stand rigid like a tall oak that cracks and collapses in the storm. Instead, you want to be flexible, like a reed that bends with the storm and survives."

– Deepak Chopra

I generally regard the world—and my life in particular—as a place to watch, wonder, and learn. I guess that's why the Universe continues to send me so many lessons about dealing with difficult people!

One important lesson involved my own daughter—my oldest, who is 13 years old. She is a wonderful young lady, and I feel blessed to be her mom. But lately, she finds fault with absolutely everything I do. She gives me a lot of opportunities to practice what I preach, as she presents herself to me as a difficult person in my own home to deal with each day.

I call my daughter "difficult" because I never know whether I'm going to be thanked for doing something right or skewered for doing something wrong—in her opinion. In fact, from day to day, I'm never quite sure what will make her happy—or upset.

I realized that much of my defensiveness when dealing with my daughter, or even my emotional outrage, comes from my belief that she "should respect" me as her mother. Now, maybe she should, but because I color all of our interactions with the you'd-better-respect-me filter, I focus more on my need for respect than her need to act out.

Sometimes my "respect" filter goes up the second she walks into a room. I have to literally force myself to step outside our interactions and watch what's happening between us. When I can adopt an observer role, I'm amazed at how much more smoothly our interactions go. I think I usually have a mental wall between us that screams "respect me!" and I stand ready for her to act out defiantly. When I drop my guard and my need for her respect, she seems to drop her "full speed ahead" attitude in response.

I've discovered that, many times, I might be a bit too quick to dispense criticism. After all, I AM the mom. But honestly, my child is as much my teacher as I am hers. When I am open to her, I learn a lot. I realize that I have as much to learn as she does. We become equal.

* EXERCISES *

Today, leave your filters in your dresser drawer. Seek out someone you often find difficult — like your child, spouse, parent, sibling, coworker, etc. — and let THEM teach YOU. It is not easy, but it is very gratifying when a relationship strengthens as a result of the effort.

Remove your filters long enough to consider the opinions, beliefs, and experiences of others. You may learn something!

Write about a situation during which your opinions, beliefs, and experiences colored an interaction with someone. What could you have done differently? Why?

* 60-DAY OPTION *

Tomorrow, apply what you can do differently to let someone else's opinions, experiences, and/or beliefs teach you something.

a couple more

Well, four weeks is only 28 days, and I promised that I'd help you understand other people in 30 days, not four weeks, so I owe you a couple more tips. If you have successfully stayed with this program, you'll definitely want to keep going and make it a full month.

I am often reminded of the power of self-talk and how the same words can, under varying circumstances, mean vastly different things. Here's an example: I was going to an early-morning client meeting, and I knew I'd hit rush hour traffic. Where I live, rush hour traffic is something to be avoided at all costs. I allowed extra time for my commute, knowing that I would need it.

After driving for about 45 minutes, I found myself stuck in gridlock traffic. I later learned that there had been an accident on a one-lane road up ahead, but as I sat in a sea of idling cars, I couldn't know what was happening. I found myself sneaking desperate looks at the clock on my dashboard. The meeting was scheduled for 9 a.m., and the clock now read "8:01".

I thought, "I have only one hour to get there. It is already 8, and I only have until 9 to start this meeting." I realized that I was beginning to get very panicky sitting in my car and thinking "only one hour," "just one hour."

All of a sudden, I realized what I was doing, and I changed the tone of my thoughts immediately: "I have one entire hour. I don't have to be there for one whole hour. I have an hour left to go only a short distance." As I changed my self-talk, the "short" one hour turned into a much longer period of time.

Whether it is "only an hour" or "a whole hour" makes a world of difference. The hour is the same, but the two different interpretations make that hour the shortest one in the world or the longest one.

This incident reminded me how powerful words can be, depending on how we apply them and how we use them — for or against ourselves. I could choose to continue to use my self-talk to make myself more and more agitated as I sat there unable to move, or I could turn it around and calm myself by feeling confident and taking life a second at a time. Becoming agitated would have made that ride so much more difficult. Calming myself down was a lot more beneficial!

In the end, I was able to get to the meeting with 10 minutes to spare. That hour was ample time. It's a great reminder, though, to watch the self-talk and to err on the side of the positive whenever possible. As one of my colleagues likes to say, "If you're going to make something up in your mind, you may as well make up something positive!"

As you go through the next couple of exercises, remember that you have the power to change your interpretation of just about anything. It's your choice!

day | twenty | - | nine

is | winning | everything | ?

"Winning takes talent; to repeat
takes character."

– John Wooden

One summer, my son and my nephew went to baseball camp together. My nephew is an amazing athlete—we've always marveled at how agile and capable he is, even as a young child, and he continues to develop beyond our wildest dreams. At the baseball camp there were "contests" for the fastest runner round the bases, the best infielder, and the best outfielder. Technically, my nephew won two of the three contests but he was "only allowed to win one," so they took the other win away from him.

As a mother I can relate to the desire to teach kids that life isn't all about winning; it should be about doing your best. Don't all mothers want their kids to be a "success" at whatever they choose to do? Hearing my nephew calmly talk about how he had to say he was disqualified, in order for the other "winner" to save face, I also thought about how unfair it is to take an award away from a child because he, or she, is more proficient than others in more than one area.

When children get out into the real world, the truth is that there are those who get the gold ring and those who don't. There ARE winners and then there are people who compete but who don't get the winning ticket. We can't deny this and protect our kids from the pain of loss for their entire lives. But no parent wants their kids to feel hurt or defeated, and we often try and protect them for as long as we can!

After the incident with my nephew, I polled a few people on their viewpoint about what had happened. There were two clear camps—often it was the moms who thought it was nice that others had a chance to win, and often it was the dads who felt it was preposterous that an award could be taken from a child who worked for it and deserved it. What was interesting to me was the passion with which a parent could debate their position on the topic.

It's a good reminder about how often we view things as black and white—or right and wrong. I can honestly say I see both sides of the discussion and think both have merit. I probably come down more firmly on the side of wanting the true winner to have both awards if that is what they earned, but maybe my view is colored because in this case it was my nephew!

* EXERCISES *

Today, observe how you engage in an inner or outer dialogue about what's "right" or "fair" and what's not. We become so attached to our own point of view that we sometimes fail to realize it is still our view, and others are also entitled to their own separate opinions, even though we may disagree. Be aware of the tendency to label the other person "bad" or "wrong;" instead, think of it as simply a difference in viewpoint.

We all realize that not everyone shares the same opinions as we do. But when it comes to interacting with others, we do tend to split off into groups of like-minded individuals. Especially in groups; we then tend to label opposing groups of individuals "wrong" or "bad." In our heart of hearts, we know that these folks aren't bad; they're just different.

Write about a situation during which you automatically labeled someone "wrong" or "bad" because they didn't share the same opinions or beliefs as you. What could you have done differently? Why?

* 60-DAY OPTION *

Tomorrow, apply what you can do differently to let others have their own opinions and/or beliefs.

day | thirty
review|ing | resolution s

"I think in terms of the day's resolutions,
not the year's."

– Henry Moore

was recently interviewed by the *Christian Science Monitor, SheKnows. com*, and *Opposing Views* about Charlie Sheen and his rather erratic behavior. The focus of these interviews was on how we can make change stick if we want to move from one form of behavior to another—in Charlie's case, a more positive form!

Making real change happen is often difficult. Most people get to early March before they realize that the New Year's resolutions they excitedly made about eight weeks previously have not produced any real change in their lives. Those of us who failed at yet another resolution end up feeling like "What's wrong with me? Why can't I ever make a shift? Why don't I do what I want to do?" We feel like failures… and then we go back to our old ways of doing things.

Most of the time, we make a resolution, and even after we realize we've failed, we desire to change—as Charlie Sheen, for example, may or may not want to; we are motivated and believe we are committed, but maybe we aren't really focused on where we want to go. We know that where we are isn't good, but we're not sure about the next place we need to be. All we know is, we want to get away from where we are!

There are two reasons we try to shift our position—we either want to move away from the place we're in, or we want to move toward a new place and new situation. The problem is that when we are looking to get away, to flee from our current undesirable state, we sometimes don't know what that "greener grass" really looks like from the other side. We make a move, but then we find ourselves stuck because we don't really know where we are going—or because we fear what it will look like when we get there.

Understanding what really matters is an important key in any change process. Why am I making this move now? What do I care about? What would success look like to me? How will I know when I have reached my desired outcome? How will I feel? What will be happening there?

Doing for the sake of doing, and changing for the sake of changing, isn't always very practical. Sure, the mere experience of acting on a change makes us feel good—as if we are moving in SOME direction—but how many times do we find that we actually went in a circle and wound up back where we started from? We start running, and put a lot of energy into our new change, and then wake up one day wondering "How the heck did I get here?"

* EXERCISES *

Having a clear picture of what we want and what it looks like to us is helpful. Today, on a 3 × 5 card, write down what you want to achieve. I'd recommend starting with a short-term goal—maybe something you can get done today or this week. Keep the card close; in your wallet or purse, or taped to a wall is good. Taking the time to record what you want, to envision it and to ensure that it really is where you want to go, is often the first step in making a real change.

Bonus: If you're really committed to making a change, get a journal and keep track of each step you make toward a goal. Write down each step and check it off when you get there. Motivation and commitment are great—but make sure you are coupling them with a clear focus about what that end state looks like to you!

Make a list of goals that you want to eventually cover on your cards. Today, you'll begin with one goal, a small one, but as you achieve more and more, you'll want to come back to this list and check off more of your achievements.

* 60-DAY OPTION *

Tomorrow, review past "resolutions" you made. What obstacles did you encounter in making a change happen? Can you revive any of them and try a new and different approach?

lesson s | from
our | furry | friend s

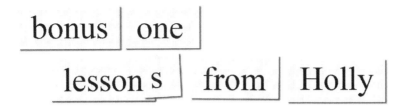

bonus | one
lesson s | from | Holly

> "Pets are humanizing. They remind us we have an obligation and responsibility to preserve and nurture and care for all life."
>
> – James Cromwell

I am a serious animal lover. I have 10 pets of my own, and I often foster abandoned animals. I volunteer at the local rescue group every Monday, cleaning cages. The animals are very, very special to me.

We adopted a beautiful kitten last February—the first kitten I have ever had; I had always adopted grown cats. Holly came into our lives and was immediately the Princess of our home. Her personality was larger than life, and she made us laugh. One weekend—while we were away and our pet sitter was at our house—there was a tragic accident at our home and Holly was killed.

My husband and I have had a difficult time recovering. We both cried quite a bit and really struggled to get past her death. One morning over coffee—and tears—we decided to talk about the gifts that Holly brought us and what we learned from her. I decided to share these with the hope that we can all learn from spirited, beautiful Holly. What lessons did she offer as her gifts?

1. **Kindness.** With nine other animals in the house, someone is always

fighting with someone else. Holly embraced everyone: She loved the dogs. She loved the other cats. She was always sleeping next to someone, cleaning them, or following them around. Instead of saying, "I don't know about those other pets, let me stand apart from them," she just threw herself into new relationships and found common ground with everyone.

2. **Don't worry—be happy.** Holly was always finding a cat tree to climb, a ball to play with, a bug to chase, or a sunny spot to bask in. She thrived wherever she was. Life was filled with all kinds of things to explore and enjoy. She never cried or sulked—purring was her middle name!

3. **Show love.** Holly had a special fondness for my husband. He was the only one who could hold her busy little body for any period of time. She sat on his sweater by his computer and tilted her little head to communicate with him during the workday. She followed him everywhere, climbed into his pants as he was putting them on in the morning, and purred contentedly as she slept near him each night. He said he could feel the unconditional love emanating from her all the time—and it felt good.

4. **Peace and contentment.** Holly was so peaceful even in the midst of household strife. The kids could yell and scream, the dogs could bark, and the other cats could get into cat fights, and little Holly would just lie in the middle of the floor looking like "life is grand!" She didn't get ruffled by the things that happened around her; she had an aura of peace and contentment that helped the rest of us get a grip when the commotion level increased.

5. **Have fun!** Holly's greatest gift might have been to remind us that life can be fun whenever we want it to be. Everything was a game to her: Getting ready for bed at night was fun. Having meals was exciting. Our coming into and leaving the house was reason to run around and rejoice. Her fun and upbeat spirit made us smile constantly. That spirit permeated everything we did and lifted our hearts no matter what else was going on. During difficult times, we could just turn and look at happy Holly to get our center back.

The hole Holly left is still wide open and very painful. Even with many other animals and beautiful children in my home, there is an emptiness left behind. But with the blessings that Holly bestowed upon us, we are hoping to take her lessons and apply them to every minute of our days.

* EXERCISES *

Today, think of Holly, or a furry friend who has made an impact in your own life.

List a situation during which you were unkind or worried, refused to show love, were not at peace or content, and didn't have any fun—list one situation for each of these. What could you have done differently in each situation to be kind, unworried, loving, at peace, and having fun? Why?

* 60-DAY OPTION *

Tomorrow, apply what you can do differently to be more like Holly.

bonus | two

shake | it | off | !

One day a farmer's donkey fell into an abandoned well. The animal cried piteously for hours as the farmer tried to figure out what to do. Finally, he decided the animal was old and the well needed to be covered up anyway, so it just wasn't worth it to him to try to retrieve the donkey.

He invited all his neighbors to come over and help him. They each grabbed a shovel and began to shovel dirt into the well. Realizing what was happening, the donkey at first cried and wailed horribly. Then, a few shovelfuls later, he quieted down completely.

The farmer peered down into the well, and was astounded by what he saw. With every shovelful of dirt that hit his back, the donkey was doing something amazing. He would shake it off and take a step up on the new layer of dirt. As the farmer's neighbors continued to shovel dirt on top of the animal, he would shake it off and take a step up.

Pretty soon, the donkey stepped up over the edge of the well and trotted off, to the shock and astonishment of all the neighbors. Life is going to shovel dirt on you, all kinds of dirt. The trick to getting out of the well is to not let it bury you, but to shake it off and take a step up. Each of our troubles is a stepping stone.

We can get out of the deepest wells just by not stopping,
never giving up! Shake it off and take a step up!

– Unknown

Although I am very fortunate to have a job I love and to work with wonderful and talented people every day, my favorite part of the week is cleaning the dog cages at the rescue group based in my hometown. Every Monday morning, I am there to take each pup out of his or her cage, clean up, refresh the food and water, and then put the little one back in. Of course, I always manage to have some cuddle time, too—that's the best part!

Almost all of these dogs come to the shelter with some kind of sad or tragic story. Many were abandoned, abused, starved, or dumped. One pregnant mom we had two weeks ago had been left locked in a house after her family had moved away. The stories are endless. But as I walk in the door every Monday, I am greeted with a cacophony of barks, whines, and wags. When each cage door gets opened, the canine inhabitant either bounds into my arms or shrinks back afraid until I pick him up, or take her out, and show them it is okay.

No matter what these animals have been through, they are still capable of showing an abundance of love and affection to any person who will come along and feed them, hold them, and show them some compassion. They readily give their unconditional attention and love to people even though they've been so mistreated.

Why can't people have that same "dog-spirit" toward other people? Why, when someone does us wrong, do we hold on to it, keep it close, and build a wall between ourselves and that person and other people? I'm not suggesting that someone stay with someone who is abusive (even the dogs got away!) or that we allow someone who is hurtful to continue to hurt us, but why do we have to hold on to the hurt even when we escape the situation? Why do we experience a bad day, or a difficult confrontation, and then inflict our feelings on the next person we interact with? In many cases, family members know the minute we walk through the door that we have had "a bad day" because we let them know about it—even though they may have had nothing to do with it.

At times, we could all benefit from having a shorter memory span, like dogs. What if every time someone did us wrong, we simply shook it off and licked the face (metaphorically speaking, of course) of the next person we saw, instead of holding on to our hurt or anger? The ability to emotionally move past someone who has hurt us and turn our attention to happier and more uplifting things is lost to so many people. We allow ourselves to stew and wallow, and continue to let the anger or hurt churn inside.

At times, I find myself thinking about someone who has done something wrong, especially to my children, and wanting to "fix it" and make it right. But when I step back and observe what I am doing, I realize that I am actually hurting my children more by continuing to churn and burn over what happened. Instead of focusing on my kids with a happy spirit, I am busy making plans to write a letter, or make a call and tell someone off.

When I realize what I am doing, and simply let go of the need to let the negativity live on, all of my relationships benefit.

* EXERCISES *

Today — think like a dog. Even if you aren't a dog lover, you may be able to appreciate the unconditional nature of the dog spirit. Try to shake off whatever (or whoever!) is holding you back. I find it helpful to literally stand up and shake my whole body to rid myself of the toxic ideas I am carrying around. Give it a try!

Whether you decide to give yourself a good figurative or literal shake, remember that we all let far too much of what goes on around us get to us. Just because you run into someone who is determined to behave badly doesn't mean you have to let it ruin your day. Don't give control of your day to anyone else. YOU decide how your day will play out.

Write about a situation during which you were unable to let go of something relatively minor. What could you have done differently? Why?

* 60-DAY OPTION *

Tomorrow, apply what you can do differently to just shake it off!

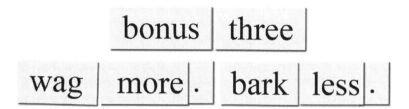

bonus three
wag more. bark less.

"How far you go in life depends on your being tender with the young, compassionate with the aged, sympathetic with the striving and tolerant of the weak and strong. Because someday in your life you will have been all of these."

– George Washington Carver

Driving my kids to school one morning, I found myself at a stop light behind a van with this bumper sticker: "Wag More. Bark Less." Being an animal lover and one who is very involved in dog rescue, I smiled as I thought of the image behind it. But more importantly, it made me stop in my mental tracks. As we had been getting ready that morning, struggling to get to school on time (an ongoing challenge in my household), I realized how much I had been "barking" and how little I had been "wagging" as I ushered my children through their morning.

If we think about every hour of the day—how much time do we spend wagging versus barking? How often do we share joy and excitement with the people around us, versus cussing or complaining? Some people are admittedly much better at wagging than others. I wag a lot on days we don't have to get ready for school, and seem to bark a lot on those hurried days that we have to be out the door by 6:30 a.m. with everyone fed and dressed and backpacks filled with supplies for the day!

But the bumper sticker reminded me of how important it is to recognize how much I held the key to my emotional response to the rushing we had been doing that morning. I had a choice not to devolve into a complaining mother, sighing and getting aggravated at my children as they came out the door late to get to school. I had the option, even in the midst of the chaos, to wag and smile. They needed to get to school on time, but I could hurry them along with a different attitude.

Why can dogs and other animals bounce back from difficulty, but as humans, we hold on to our frustration, anger, and impatience and won't let a smile curve our lips when we want to show the other person just how irritated we are at their behavior? I've found that sometimes the best way to bring myself back to a positive state, or to break a tension, is to laugh in the middle of my own frustration, to take an unbiased look at what I am doing and realize how silly and unnecessary it is.

I've had times where I was in a "stand-off" with one of my kids over something and we were both ready to dig our heels in, then someone will inadvertently laugh or make a joke and we both end up laughing at our own silliness. It gives us a chance to look at the impasse a bit more objectively and without so much negative emotion.

Isn't it a wonderful experience to be somewhere and someone you don't know wags at you: They smile, they greet you openly, or they just say "Hello"? It's hard to walk away without a smile on my face when someone does this for me.

I actually made up a little sign for my computer: "Wag More. Bark Less." so I could be reminded of how important this idea really is. Often, as I type, I have my four dogs (and several cats) snoring nearby, so that small reminder makes it a little easier for me to remember how easy it is to bask in the enjoyment of life, rather than barking at all of the little things that intrude upon our day.

* EXERCISES *

Today, perfect your wag in the midst of trouble and silence your bark when there is really nothing you'd like to do more! Put a smile on your face even if things aren't perfect. Smile at a perfect stranger and say "Hello!" Tell someone to have a great day. Pay someone an unsolicited compliment.

Write about a situation during which you barked when you could have wagged. What could you have done differently? How would that have changed the situation?

* 60-DAY OPTION *

Tomorrow, apply what you can do differently to wag more and bark less.

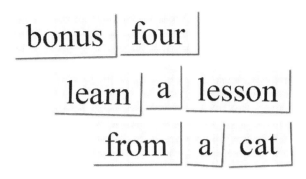

bonus four
learn a lesson
from a cat

"No one can get inner peace by pouncing on it."

– Harry Emerson Fosdick

It isn't easy for most of us to step outside of ourselves and truly observe what's happening in life and with other people. Our minds race, and often we want to jump in and let someone know what we think about what they are saying or doing. Most of us, though, want to increase our communication with others—and strengthen our relationships. The best way to do this is to stay still and be aware of what's happening with us and with others.

I, like many people, struggle with exactly how to stop myself and stay still and focused on another person. I practice being an Interested Observer quite a bit each day, but I am always looking for other ways to improve. Today I found my tutors—my cats!

As I was making breakfast this morning, I was watching how very still and silent one of my cats was being as he watched the birds outside the window. It was as if he were a statue, he was so focused and intent on the view. As he sat there I marveled at the incredible fortitude and patience that a cat shows when they want to. There was nothing we could do to move him from his vantage point—call his name, throw a treat on the floor, or wiggle his favorite feather. He was rooted to that spot, just watching and waiting.

Now, I hope we don't learn to "pounce" on other people as my cat would likely do if I let him out with the birds! But the stillness and the calm centeredness he displayed are what I strive for in my relationships with others. Being still and allowing the other person to reveal themselves, what they care about and what is going on with them, is the kindest and most loving thing we can do for another. Most of us just want to be understood—and deep down few of us think that we are, even by those that love us. Being patient and non-judgmental is such a gift we can offer to another person.

* EXERCISES *

Today, practice a bit being still. I know I am always moving, often rushing, and many times during the day I need to remind myself to "slow down." Strength comes from stillness, and a few times each day we need to stop what we are doing, watch our triggers with others, and give ourselves more choice about how we engage.

Become a people watcher. Dedicate yourself to listening, not speaking. Spend time doing something someone else wants to do. Hold hands with a loved one.

Write about a situation during which you pounced instead of remaining calm. What could you have done differently? Why?

* 60-DAY OPTION *

Tomorrow, apply what you can do differently to be still.

ABOUT THE AUTHOR

Beverly D. Flaxington, two-time bestselling and Gold Award-winning author, is an accomplished consultant, hypnotherapist, personal and career coach, author, college professor, corporate trainer, facilitator, behavioral expert, entrepreneur, and business development expert.

Beverly's knowledge of human behavior and the most effective ways to make change happen have helped thousands of people and hundreds of organizations over the years. She is an entrepreneur, having founded two very successful businesses. Her consulting firm, The Collaborative (www.the-collaborative.com), works with organizations of all shapes and sizes to help them meet and beat their goals and improve working relationships between staff and management.

She is a frequent speaker and contributor to articles on the subjects of sales, marketing, behavioral issues, employee and career issues, effective time management, and dealing with difficult people. Bev has been quoted hundreds of times including in *The Wall Street Journal*, *The Boston Globe*, *U.S. News & World Report*, and Foxnews.com. She is frequently interviewed on radio and television.

Beverly authored the bestselling and Gold Award-winning *Understanding Other People: The Five Secrets to Human Behavior* (www.understandingotherpeople.com). She authored the bestselling *Make Your SHIFT: The Five Most Powerful Moves You Can Make to Get Where YOU Want to Go*. The business companion is *Make the SHIFT: The Proven Five-Step Plan to Success for Corporate Teams*. She also authored *The 7 Steps to Effective Business Building for Financial Advisors: How top earning advisors attract and retain the most profitable clients* and the companion Workbook for this program. The 7 Steps program was selected by the Financial Planning Association and is available in their online store at a member discount.

Beverly is an adjunct professor at Suffolk University. She teaches "Leadership and Social Responsibility," a required course where *Make the SHIFT* is a required text. Beverly is a Certified Hypnotist, Certified Hypnosis Trainer, Reiki Master Attunement Practitioner, Certified Professional Behavioral Analyst (CPBA), and Certified Professional Values Analyst (CPVA).

Contact Bev today to learn additional ways to improve your relationships! Visit www.understandingotherpeople.com

Made in the USA
Middletown, DE
27 July 2017